psychology

psychology

adventures in perception
and personality

christian jarrett & joannah ginsburg

METRO BOOKS
NEW YORK

METRO BOOKS
New York

An Imprint of Sterling Publishing
1166 Avenue of the Americas
New York, NY 10036

Conceived, designed, and produced by
Quid Publishing
Level 4, Sheridan House
114 Western Road
Hove BN3 1DD
England

Interior layout and illustrations by Tony Seddon

ISBN 978-1-4351-5472-8

For information about custom editions, special sales, and premium and corporate purchases,
please contact Sterling Special Sales at 800-805-5489 or specialsales@sterlingpublishing.com.

Manufactured in China

2 4 6 8 10 9 7 5 3

www.sterlingpublishing.com

CONTENTS

WHAT IS PSYCHOLOGY?

Let's start with what psychology is not. Psychology isn't mind reading or mere common sense. Psychology is not only concerned with people who have mental health problems. And psychology isn't just about body language. Psychology is a diverse science of the mind and of behavior, as well as a thriving applied profession.

Since the dawn of the world's ancient civilizations in China, India, Egypt, and Greece, great thinkers have been asking questions about the nature of the human mind and why people behave the way that they do. But it is only relatively recently that scholars have taken a scientific approach to these issues, thus heralding the birth of psychology (literally the "study of the mind," from the Greek psyche, meaning mind or soul, and logos, meaning study or discourse).

A scientific approach means forming predictions, observing, and testing those predictions, before replicating the whole exercise again for good measure. Verification, control, reliability, counting, watching, explaining—this is really what it's all about.

Anyone can make a claim about human behavior: "If you smile, it makes you feel happier," but only psychologists will go about testing that claim with careful, precise experiments. They'll recruit participants and devise sensitive ways to measure mood. They'll consider possible "confounds"—for instance, perhaps any kind of exercise of the facial muscles improves mood? The psychologists won't leave this to chance. They'll make sure

they test not only the effects of smiling but also the impact of frowning or chewing.

Probably the earliest person to investigate mental processes in a scientific way was Wilhelm Wundt, who founded the world's first psychology lab in Leipzig in 1879—the Insitut für Experimentelle Psychologie. Wundt sought to break consciousness down into its constituent parts, an endeavor that came to be known as Structuralism. Although Wundt's approach brought new levels of precision to the study of the mind, he still employed the philosophical technique of introspection which, because of its subjective nature, is today not seen as very scientific.

The new century witnessed the dawn of a new field of psychology—behaviorism—which sought to be as rigorously scientific as possible. Its founder, the U.S. psychologist John Watson, and its later proponents including B.F. Skinner, believed psychology could only claim to be a science if it focused strictly on outwardly observable behavior. Their influence meant that it was only by the middle of the twentieth century that experimental psychologists, inspired by developments in computer science, began to focus once again on mental processes.

Areas of Psychology

Social psychology seeks to understand how we interact with each other and looks at issues like group processes, prejudice, and embarrassment. Developmental psychology tends to focus on the learning and maturation of infants and children but also investigates the ways in which we change throughout our lives. Cognitive psychology is concerned with information processing: how we perceive the world, move in it, remember it, and talk about it. Cognitive neuropsychology looks at how brain damage affects these mental faculties. Comparative psychology considers animal behavior and views our own antics in an evolutionary context. There's biological psychology which investigates how our physical bodies affect the way we behave, including studying functions like sleeping and stress. Occupational psychology studies behavior at work, while health psychology looks at our response to illness. There's individual differences research that focuses on personality and intelligence and all the ways in which we vary from one another. Of course many psychologists also study mental illness, including depression, anxiety, and psychosis, and they measure the effectiveness of psychological treatments for these conditions.

On top of all that, there are also the more recent domains of psychology, including environmental psychology, which, as you might guess, tackles the ways in which the environment affects our behavior and how we affect it. There's parapsychology which studies anomalous experiences, and criminological psychology which strives to understand criminal behavior, as well as the behavior of juries and police techniques. One of the newest areas of the discipline is positive psychology which aims to understand human growth and achievement with the same fervor as has previously been directed at studying human misery and suffering.

Modern Psychological Techniques

Many psychological techniques have changed little over the years. You still can't beat asking someone how they feel or what they believe about something. Psychologists continue to do just that using carefully validated questionnaires and structured interviews. But probably the biggest change in psychology research over the last couple of decades has come from the development of brain imaging techniques like magnetic resonance imaging (MRI) and positron emission tomography (PET). These still don't provide a direct measure of human thought as some commentators might have you believe, but they do provide a window into the biological workings of the mind. Another relatively new technique is transcranial magnetic stimulation (TMS) which allows psychologists to temporarily knock out the functioning in a region of a healthy person's brain, so inducing what's often dubbed a "virtual" lesion.

Types of Applied Psychologist

As the science of psychology beavers away uncovering what makes us tick, many psychologists take what we've learned so far out into the world for the betterment of society. Clinical and counseling psychologists use evidence-based therapeutic techniques to help people with mental problems. Business psychologists help companies improve productivity and staff morale. Forensic psychologists help rehabilitate offenders and advise the police. Educational psychologists help children at school, especially those with learning difficulties. Sports psychologists work with teams and athletes,to help them reach their peak performance. Meanwhile, health psychologists help people cope with illness and advise on health care and promotion.

Buckle up and get comfy—you're about to be taken on a roller-coaster ride through popular psychology:

Perception and Action takes a look at how we're plugged into the world via our senses and includes some neat illusions that show how our brains sometimes make mistakes.

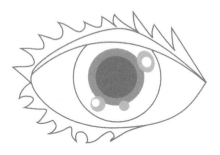

Memory takes a journey through our mental archives, including some tips on boosting your memory abilities and a survey of recent research on whether bad memories can be erased.

Cognition gets inside your mind, showing you're not as rational as you thought and looking at problems some people have with language and counting.

Affect may challenge some of your basic ideas on human behavior and communication patterns, exploring animal instincts and personality traits.

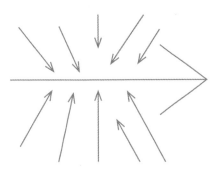

Stress and Anxiety shows the strange ways our brains and bodies can react when we are faced with especially intense or traumatic situations.

The Social Self recognizes that we're social beings, rounds up research on relationships, as well as putting leadership and brainstorming under the microscope.

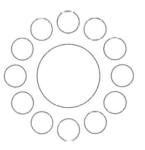

Personality puts the spotlight on you, with a range of tests that should help you get to know yourself better.

Sleep explores the fascinating and complicated relationship of mind and body, helping us understand what we may learn about ourselves through our dreams, explaining phenomena such as sleepwalking and narcolepsy, and providing tips on how to be more in touch with your dreaming self and how to get better sleep!

Throughout the chapters you'll find mini features on some key psychologists who have worked in these fields. At the end of the book there's a handy index of notable psychologists mentioned throughout the text, as well as a selected bibliography of some of the main works we've cited.

Chapter

1

Perception and Action

Our sensory pathways communicate a whirlwind
of data about the world to the brain, which is
essentially a meaty information processing
machine. This chapter, covering vision, hearing,
touch, and more, is about how the brain makes
sense of all that information and uses it to
decide how to act. But everything is not always
as it seems, as we'll discover with illusions
and other phenomena.

SEEING

As you glance about enjoying all the richness of the visual world, it is easy to underestimate the complex journey that makes sight possible. It starts with light rays hitting a screen of photo-receptive cells at the back of your eyes—the retina—where the light is turned into a neural signal. Next comes the optic nerve, which carries the visual information on to a relay station, the lateral geniculate nucleus, from where it is wired to the sprawling visual cortex at the back of your brain. Something curious about the wiring of the visual system is that it's actually the left-hand side of your brain that processes the right side of space, and the right-hand side of your brain that processes the left half.

The Science of Sight

Beyond the first stage of the visual cortex, known as primary visual cortex or V1, the processing of visual information is effectively split into two parts, for the purposes of either performing actions or perceiving what things are. This has been demonstrated through the observation of patients with damage to one pathway or the other. For example, the psychologists David Milner and Melvyn Goodale described the case of patient D.F., who, with her damaged "perception" stream, was unable to say which way a post-box type slot was orientated, yet was perfectly capable of "posting" letters into the slot by angling her delivery correctly.

Light-sensitive cells on your retina are not distributed evenly but are concentrated in the center, in a region called the fovea. This is one of the reasons you need to move your eyes around, so that you can focus objects of interest on this high-acuity foveal region. There are also two types of retinal cells—rods for seeing shades of gray in dim light, and cones for processing color. Rods tend to be concentrated more in the periphery of your retina which is why, in the dark, you might actually find it easier to see something by looking just to one side of it rather than straight on.

Eye Movements

The eye movement you make most often is called a saccade. These are the jerky, jumpy movements people make when they are reading. A little-known fact is that when you move your eyes in this way, your vision is actually shut down temporarily, to stop the visual scene blurring with the thousands of these movements you make every day. Because saccadic eye movements are so fast, typically lasting less than a quarter of a second, you don't usually notice this effect, but there is an illusion, called the "Stopped Clock Effect," which some experts have suggested is caused by this brief visual shut-down.

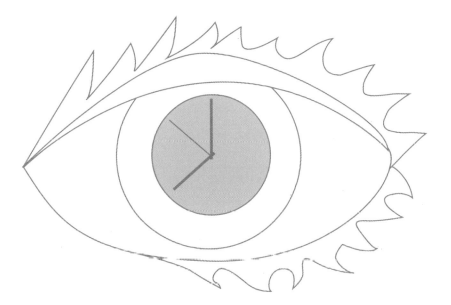

TRY OUT THE "STOPPED CLOCK EFFECT"

Find a clock—an old-fashioned one with hands is better, as long as it doesn't tick, but a digital one will also do so long as it shows seconds. Now place the clock to one side and glance over at the second hand (or digits). The clock must be far enough away so that you have to shift your eyes to see it. You might need to try this a few times, but hopefully you should eventually notice that the second hand seems to hang still for too long, almost as though the clock has stopped momentarily.

One explanation for why this happens is that, in order to compensate for the visual suppression that occurs during eye movements, your brain effectively back-dates how long it believes an object has been in its current position. This works fine when you glance at an inanimate object like a desk or book, but it can cause a strange sensation when you glance at an object like a second hand which you know ought not to be in one place for too long.

WATCHING THINGS MOVE

Being able to see when things are moving is vital to our survival. We wouldn't have lasted long on the open savannah if we hadn't been able to notice that lion jumping toward us, or our potential dinner running off.

What Is Motion?

Motion is literally a change in position over time, and you detect movement when the image of an object or animal moves across the cells of your retina. However, there are all sorts of complicated computations involved in motion perception because, to tell whether other things are moving, you have to factor in your own movements—both those of your entire body through space, and also of your eyes.

Usually when you move your eyes, the motor command for the eye movement is copied and used to cancel out any consequential movement of images across the retina. However, if you move one of your eyes using a gentle nudge of your finger against your eyeball, you'll see that in this case the world does appear to move. This is because you moved your eye externally with your finger, so there wasn't an internal "eye movement command" to cancel out.

Motion Blindness

In 1983, Joseph Zihl and colleagues described the case of a 43-year-old woman, referred to as L.M., who lost the ability to see motion (known as akinetopsia) after suffering strokes on both sides of her brain. Her impairment was strikingly specific, as she retained her ability to recognize objects and words, and could even detect the movement of sounds through space, or the movement of an object up and down her arm.

L.M.'s story reminds us just how important our ability to see movement is. She couldn't pour out drinks because the fluid just appeared frozen in mid-air, and as you can imagine, crossing the road was particularly hazardous. Her highly selective impairment also tells us that the processing of visual motion must be carried out in a specialized way in the brain. Indeed her strokes caused damage to a region of her brain—an area now referred to by psychologists as visual area V5, at the junction of the parietal, occipital, and temporal lobes—that modern brain-imaging techniques have shown is selectively activated when we look at motion.

The Waterfall Illusion

There are plenty of fun illusions that each reveal something different about the way we process motion. Probably the oldest and most famous of these is known as the "waterfall illusion." If you haven't got a waterfall handy, you need to find something large that is constantly moving in one direction, like a luggage carousel or a river flowing by.

Stare at the waterfall for a good 30 seconds or so and then look away. You'll see that the rocks to the side of the fall appear to be rushing upward in the opposite direction to the waterfall. It's thought that this effect is caused by cells sensitive to the downward direction of the waterfall becoming desensitized. Normally, cells sensitive to different directions are in a kind of balanced opposition, but once the downwardly sensitive cells are fatigued by the waterfall, the upwardly sensitive cells dominate and lead us to perceive upward motion that isn't really there.

The Flash Lag Effect

One problem when it comes to perceiving moving objects is the fact that it takes a certain amount of time for neural signals carrying visual information to travel through the brain. So by the time we've finished processing a moving object in its current position, it will actually be somewhere else further along its trajectory. This effect is strikingly demonstrated in a phenomenon known as the "Flash Lag Effect" in which a briefly flashed stationary object appears to lag behind its moving partner, even though both objects are really in alignment.

It's difficult to recreate this effect at home, but you can find some examples on the internet if you do a web search. If you were feeling really ambitious you could try attaching a camera securely to a piece of string or rope. Put the flash on and use the delay function for taking photos of yourself. Now watch the camera as you spin it around in a circle. Hopefully, as the flash goes off it should appear to lag behind the actual camera. Make sure you try this in daylight, because if you do it in the dark you get visual after-effects from the flash that will confuse things.

One explanation for this effect is that in order to compensate for neural processing

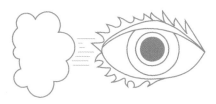

delays, our brains actually locate moving objects slightly ahead of their true position. This process isn't applied to stationary objects, hence the way the stationary, flashed object appears to lag behind the moving one. Psychologists have even argued that the effect could be responsible for some incorrect off-side judgments in soccer.

The Falling Man

Another related phenomenon reported by psychologists concerns stationary images that imply movement, and is known as Representational Momentum. Imagine looking at a still picture of a man jumping off a building. Researchers have shown that our mental representation of this image is dynamic, in the sense that it continues to move, with the man represented further down his falling path. How do we know this? Well, when people are shown still pictures of this kind, and are then presented with later frames—for example with the falling man displayed lower down his drop—they will often mistakenly say that the later frame is the same as the original they were shown earlier. Crucially they don't make this mistake when shown earlier frames, which suggests their mental representation of the image has moved forward.

BLINDSPOTS AND BLINDSIGHT

We tend to think that a blind person must have something wrong with their eyes, but people with healthy eyes who suffer damage to the principal part of their brain responsible for processing vision (the primary visual cortex), can also experience what's known as "cortical blindness." In this case, part of their visual cortex will often remain intact so that they can see one half of the visual world but not the other. A curious phenomenon called "blindsight" has been observed in these patients, in which they are able to determine the characteristics of objects placed in their blind visual field, even though they report not being able to see anything there.

Studied extensively by British psychologist Lawrence Weiskrantz, a series of experiments has shown that patients with blindsight can in fact determine object color, location, shape and brightness in their blind field, and even the emotional expression of faces. The phenomenon was actually observed in monkeys first, before being studied in humans.

Because people who exhibit blindsight say they can't see anything in their blind field, their residual abilities have been revealed by asking them to guess between options—such as "Is the shape we're showing you a square or a circle?" The patients say they can't see anything there, but their guessing performance comes out as significantly better than the 50 percent accuracy you'd expect if their answers were entirely random.

Another way researchers have revealed blindsight is to see what effect a stimulus presented in a patient's blind visual field have on their response to stimuli presented to their healthy visual field. For example, if a patient was asked to respond as fast as possible to the sight of a square in their healthy field, the presentation of an identical square in their blind field should, if processed, speed their performance. And that's exactly what's been found, further suggesting that some residual visual processing still occurs in the blind half of the patient's vision.

How can this be? Potential explanations are controversial, but it's most likely that this residual visual ability relies on parts of the visual pathway that bypass the damaged primary visual cortex, and feed instead straight into subcortical visual areas, such as the superior colliculus—areas whose processing isn't accessible to consciousness. Another possibility is that these patients have islands of intact primary visual cortex underlying their residual abilities.

Visual Neglect

Another neuropsychological condition which is reminiscent of blindsight is known as visual neglect. In this case there is nothing wrong with the patients' eyes or the visual parts of their brain, but damage to the parietal cortex (usually on the right-hand side), near the crown of the head, leads them to completely ignore half of the world, on the side opposite their injury, as if it doesn't exist. For this reason, neglect is usually considered to be a deficit of what's known as spatial attention.

The condition can manifest itself in striking ways. For example, patients will shave just one side of their face or eat from just one side of their dinner plate. Asked to draw a clock, they will miss out all the numbers on one side. However, in a similar way to blindsight, there is evidence that such patients do process some aspects of the part of space which they ignore. Asked to guess whether an object presented in their affected field is the same as an object presented to their intact field, they will perform better than you'd expect if they were just guessing.

FIND YOUR OWN BLINDSPOT

In a sense, you are blind to a part of your visual world too, thanks to what is known as the blindspot or scotoma in each of your eyes. You have a blindspot because there is a gap in your retina, through which the fibers of your photo-receptive cells leave your eye to form the optic nerve. Any light falling on this area is not processed.

You'd think these fibers would be behind the photosensitive parts of the retinal cells, so that there would be no need for a gap, but in fact the fibers are in front, with the light-detecting part behind, farthest from the outside world. This means a gap is needed to channel all the fibers out of the eye into the brain.

We're not normally aware of our two blindspots because our brains "fill in" the missing information. However, you can find out where your blindspot is by closing your left eye and looking at the cross below. Stay focused on the cross, and as you move the book gradually closer to you, or further away, at some point the circle on the right will disappear.

X   **O**

TOUCH

Touch begins in our skin, which is packed with receptors that each respond to either pressure, temperature, or pain. These skin receptors feed into the spinal cord which snakes the messages up toward the brain from where our actual sensation of touch arises. We have other sensors in our muscles too—these are for what's called proprioception, which is the sense of where the parts of our body are located in space.

A still little understood aspect of touch is itch. This sensation depends on the same nerve pathways that carry pain sensations, and to many people an unreachable itch can be a real pain. In fact there have been reports of patients who experience itchiness so excruciating that they prefer the pain of scratching themselves until they bleed to the discomfort of an itch. But then itchiness seems connected to pleasure too—just think of how satisfying it is when someone scratches that nagging itch on your back.

Inside your brain, there's a voodoo-doll-like representation of your body, which is activated when the corresponding part of your real body is touched. It's like a little you in your brain, except that each body part isn't to scale. Instead, the amount of neural tissue given over to each limb, finger, or nose depends on the sensitivity of the skin on that part of your

HERE'S ONE TO TRY

You can tell how much gray matter your brain gives over to representing the different parts of your body by carrying out what's known as a "two-point discrimination test." Far less fancy than it sounds, this simply involves seeing whether you can tell if two prongs touching your skin are two separate points, or if instead they feel just like one.

Get a friend to touch two pins or pen nibs close together on your back. If they keep reducing the distance between the pins, there will come a time when, to you, it just feels like one pin. Now close your eyes and get your friend to do the same thing again on the underside of your hand— thanks to the greater sensitivity of your hand, you should find that you can feel the two separate pin pricks over a much shorter distance than you could on your back.

body. The "little you" inside your head isn't arranged quite as you are in real life either—for example, the cells that represent your feet are found near those cells that respond when your genitals are touched!

The Social Side of Touch

Increasingly, research is uncovering just how important touch can be to our psychological well-being. For example, baby orphans deprived of human contact are more likely to die than those who are held. Touch can also be persuasive. In a paper published in 2007 in the journal *Social Influence*, French psychologist Nicolas Guéguen described how three male research assistants approached 240 women in the street and asked them for their phone numbers. Among those 120 women whom the researchers touched lightly on the arm, 19 percent agreed to share their number, compared with just 10 percent of the women with whom no physical contact was made. Furthermore, when a researcher approached women in a nightclub, of those he touched lightly on the arm, 65 percent agreed to a dance, compared with just 43 percent of those he asked without making any physical contact.

The Rubber Hand Illusion

Our sense of touch is strongly affected by our sense of sight. We seem to know this instinctively—just think of how many people look away when they're having a vaccine jab. The way sight and touch work in concert can be demonstrated dramatically with the help of a rubber arm, of the kind you might find in a joke shop (a large, stuffed rubber glove could work too), a table, and two feathers. Place your real arm underneath the table so you can't

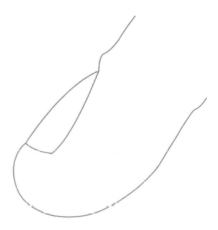

see it. Then place the rubber arm on the table, parallel with your real arm, in a position that looks as realistic as possible. Now get a friend to stroke your real arm and the rubber arm with the two feathers, with the exact same rhythm and timing. If you keep watching the rubber arm being stroked, while your real arm is stroked under the table, you should eventually experience the alarming sensation that the rubber arm is in fact part of you! The illusion shows how vision can override your proprioceptive sense of where your arm is, remapping the feeling of being stroked to the location of the rubber arm.

HEARING

I presume it's very quiet on the airless moon, because sound is the vibration of air, or some other medium, which causes the ear drum at the end of your auditory canal to vibrate. This, in turn, causes the three bones of your middle ear to move to the same beat—these are the smallest bones in your body—and they pass on the noise to your inner ear, to the cochlea, where the auditory nerves are found.

Localizing sounds is a tricky business. Whereas for sight you have retinal cells that respond to light from different regions of space, and for touch you have skin receptors all over your body, when it comes to hearing you have just the two ears planted firmly on either side of your face. So to identify where sounds are coming from, your brain uses two tricks: One is to compare the loudness of a single sound as it arrives at each ear. The second is to compare the time the sound arrives. A sound from straight ahead will arrive at each ear at the same time, but a sound from the left will obviously arrive at your left ear sooner than the right, with the opposite being true for sounds from the right.

Complete deafness is extremely rare, and in general there are two types of hearing loss. Blockage to the auditory canal, or problems with the little bones of the middle ear, is known as conductive deafness and is usually easy to rectify with surgery or hearing aids. Trouble with the inner ear, however, is more difficult to remedy and is known as nerve deafness or inner-ear deafness.

Sight and Sound

On the flip side, there is increasing evidence that blind people have enhanced hearing, probably thanks to the auditory part of their brain hijacking the redundant neural tissue normally given over to seeing.

In 2007, a surprising study suggested this hearing enhancement can also occur when sighted people are deprived of vision for short periods.

Jörg Lewald and his colleagues tested the ability of twenty blindfolded participants to say which speaker, in a semi-circular bank of stereo speakers, had emitted a noise. As expected, they tended to say the sounds were more central than they really were. But then the participants sat blindfolded for 90 minutes before being tested again. After this period of sight deprivation their performance was more accurate, and similar to the performance of blind participants. Crucially, this advantage wasn't just caused by practice at the task—participants who wore a blindfold only during testing (in other words, they didn't sit blindfolded for 90 minutes in between tests) didn't show the same improvement.

THE McGURK EFFECT

We saw in the section on touch how vision can override your proprioceptive sense of where your arm is located. The McGurk effect, first described by psychologist Harry McGurk, shows how visual information can be blended with auditory information, so that what you experience reflects a sensory combination quite different from what any one sense would have told you on its own. In this illusion, the sound of a person saying one thing (for example, the sound "BA") is played over a video showing their lips saying something else (for example, "GA"), with the result that you hear them saying a mixture of the two (for example, "DA").

The McGurk Effect tricks your brain's multi-sensory strategy that in other circumstances—such as trying to listen to your friend at a noisy nightclub—helps you interpret what they're saying. If you've got a digital camera, speaker, and the right computer kit, you could make the videos you need to test this out for yourself; otherwise there are plenty of examples you can find on the web.

Related to this is a curious phenomenon described by Oliver Sacks in his wonderful book *Seeing Voices*. When the post-lingually deaf (in other words, those people who have lost their hearing after having experienced the sound of spoken language) read people's lips, they sometimes experience the sound of the words that person is speaking—so-called "phantasmal voices." Sacks suggests that they are not just imagining what the sounds are like, but rather that the sight of the lip movements is automatically translated by their brains into the corresponding sound.

Noise

You can close your eyes to the world but there's no escaping noise, a fact made strikingly clear by a study published in 2005 showing that too much noise can increase your risk of suffering a heart attack. Stefan Willich and his colleagues interviewed thousands of people and found that men who experienced more than 60 decibels of noise at home or work were 50 percent more likely to have suffered a heart attack. Among the women, the risk of heart attack increased by up to 300 percent if they reported finding the noise annoying. Somewhat worryingly, European Union legislation, for example, states that employees should be protected from noise above 80 decibels, not 60.

MOVING

Deliberate intentions to move are formed in the brain's motor cortex, a spongy strip of gray matter that runs parallel to the neural body map that's responsible for your sense of touch. The motor cortex speaks to the spinal cord and from here the message is routed via elongated neurons to the appropriate muscles of the body.

It sounds straightforward enough, but a key problem with moving successfully is overcoming the sluggishness of your nerve signals. As we discussed in the section on seeing movement, it takes time for sensory information to find its way into the brain, and added to that is the time it takes motor commands to reach your muscles. This means quite often you're not actually moving in response to the world as you see it, but rather in response to how you think it's going to be. Your brain is a guessing machine, constantly modeling possible realities and playing out simulations of what will happen if you perform different actions.

The Broken Escalator Phenomenon

A great example of your brain anticipating what movements it thinks it needs to make occurs when you're confronted by a broken escalator of the kind that seems to be popular on underground train networks around the world. Although you know the escalator is broken, your brain's auto-pilot still kicks in to compensate for the unnatural forward movement that it's expecting. But because the escalator isn't moving, the automatic commands sent to your legs and body to help keep your balance, actually end up making you wobble a little, which can feel really strange. If you haven't experienced this before, remember to look out for the sensation the next time you encounter a broken escalator (other places to find one include shopping malls or the moving walkways at airports—just make sure you're allowed to walk on them first!)

You Can't Tickle Yourself

As well as anticipating movements that you'll need to make, another trick your brain performs is to predict the outcome of your own actions. It does this to help overcome delays in sensory feedback and also to distinguish your own actions from those of other people or animals.

A clear demonstration of this comes from the fact that you can't tickle yourself. Go on, give it a try—you'll find that it's pretty ineffective. Psychologist Sarah-Jayne Blakemore has performed a number of experiments on this topic, including one in which she had participants attempt to tickle their right hand using a robotic interface controlled by their left hand. When the interface, which had soft foam on the end, and their left hand were in perfect synchrony, the sensation didn't feel at all tickly. But then the researchers introduced a delay between the movement of the left hand and the tickling action of the foam, and they found the greater the delay, the more it tickled—effectively the sensation felt more like it was being performed by someone else.

This research suggests that when you move, a copy of the motor command is created so that its consequences can be labeled as self-generated. In other words, tickling doesn't work because the resulting sensation is anticipated and canceled out. But it seems that all it takes to disrupt this process is a little time delay.

Who's In Charge Anyway?

We've already seen that your brain can take over when faced with an unusual obstacle like an escalator. But presumably "you" are in control the majority of the time, right? Well actually maybe not. A classic study conducted by Benjamin Libet suggests that our sense of deciding when to move actually comes after the neural preparation for that movement has begun.

Participants watched a second hand on a clock and made a mental note of the moment they decided to move their finger, which they duly moved. At the same time, Libet was measuring their brain activity using electroencephalography, which records electrical changes via electrodes placed on the scalp. Libet's amazing discovery was that the spike in electrical activity normally associated with preparing to make a movement actually came a good 300–500 milliseconds prior to when the participants said they had decided to move.

A SENSORY COCKTAIL

Can you imagine if words always had a certain taste? Or if numbers and letters were always tinged with color? That's exactly what life is like for people with synaesthesia, who seem to experience a crossover of their senses resulting in a cocktail of sensations.

The most common type of synaesthete is the "letter colorer," but there are also more exotic examples. Psychologist Jamie Ward described the case of one lexical-gustatory synaesthete, J.I.W., who had to coin nicknames for some of his acquaintances because their real names consistently conjured up unpleasant tastes. Other people experience smells when musical notes are played. Another man tasted shapes.

Synaesthesia was first described by Francis Galton towards the end of the nineteenth century and many of his original observations hold true today. For example, he noticed that the condition appears to run in families, suggesting that it has a genetic basis. In rare cases, synaesthesia can also be acquired through illness—for example, it's been reported in someone with optic nerve atrophy—and can be induced by taking drugs like LSD.

Historically, some experts have doubted whether synaesthetes really do have the sensory experiences they claim, a suspicion that hasn't been helped by the observation that drugs can cause a similar sensation. But a large body of evidence has now built up which overwhelmingly suggests synaesthesia is real.

For example, synaesthetes have been tested on a version of the Stroop test, which requires participants to say what ink color a letter is written in. Consider a synaesthete who says the letter "A" evokes the color red. If the synaesthesia is real, then this person should be quicker to identify when the letter "A" is written in red ink than when it is written in blue ink, because the former situation is congruent with their synaesthetic experience. And that's exactly what the studies have shown.

Psychologist Julia Nunn and her colleagues have also scanned the brains of synaesthetes for whom words were tinged with color. The researchers found that activity was indeed sparked in the part of the brain that processes color when these participants were presented with words, but not when they were played auditory tones, thus supporting their subjective claims. By contrast, when a control group of participants were tested on the same task, the color-processing part of their brain wasn't activated by the words or tones.

A Mixing of Senses or Concepts?

More recently psychologists have been putting effort into explaining the synaesthetic experience rather than testing whether or not it is genuine. This research is showing that synaesthesia might not be a purely sensory experience after all, and could have more to do with concepts.

For example, when Julia Simner and colleagues at Edinburgh University randomly tested around 1700 people, they found not only that the condition was far more common than previously expected, with one in twenty claiming synaesthetic status, but that concept-based versions were the most common. For instance, some people reported that the days of the week or the months of the year were associated with certain colors.

A recent, ingenious study used tip-of-the-tongue syndrome—in which an unusual word or person's name feels like it is just beyond your conscious reach—to test the idea that synaesthesia can be based on concepts. For this experiment Julia Simner and Jamie Ward recruited six people for whom words tended to evoke tastes. Simner and Ward showed the synaesthetes pictures of unusual objects, such as castanets (the Spanish percussion instrument) or a platypus, and on those occasions when the participants said they knew the object but couldn't quite think of the name, they were asked to note down any associated taste sensation.

Later on, when the participants were told the names of the troublesome objects that they hadn't been able to recall, the tastes they experienced matched the tastes they reported earlier for the same objects when in the tip-of-the-tongue state. For example, one woman, who couldn't think of the word "castanets," reported experiencing the taste of tuna when the word was on the tip of her tongue, the same taste she experienced later on when she was told the word. This suggests it is the concept of "castanet" that is associated with tuna in her mind, rather than the word itself.

With findings like these, psychologists have realized synaesthesia could shed light on language processes common to all of us. For example, the experiences of synaesthete J.I.W., mentioned above, have helped answer the question of whether letters of the alphabet are processed differently by the brain depending on how they are pronounced. The answer is yes. To J.I.W., a subtle "l" as in "meaL" tastes of potatoes, while a bolder "l" as in "Light" tastes of breakfast cereal.

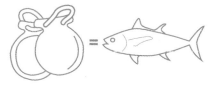

V.S. Ramachandran

Vilayanur S. Ramachandran, or "Rama" as he's affectionately known, is a behavioral neurologist renowned for his insights into the workings of the brain—many of which have come from the study of individual patients.

Born in India, Ramachandran was the son of a diplomat and raised all over the world. He originally trained as a doctor at Stanley Medical College in India before completing a Ph.D. in neurophysiology and experimental psychology at the University of Cambridge in England. Ramachandran champions the idea of taking a simple approach to solve fundamental problems, with his elegant discoveries often leaving his colleagues to wonder, "Why didn't I think of that?" He has been dubbed the Marco Polo of neuroscience by Richard Dawkins, and heralded as a modern day Paul Broca (see page 56) by Nobel laureate Eric Kandel.

Today Ramachandran wears many hats, being both Director of the Center for Brain and Cognition and Professor in the Psychology Department and Neurosciences Program at the University of California, San Diego, as well as Adjunct Professor of Biology at the Salk Institute for Biological Studies, San Diego.

Ramachandran is brimming with energy and enthusiasm and is celebrated as much for his powers of communication as for his discoveries. In 2003 he became the first doctor or psychologist to give the BBC's Reith Lectures, which were subsequently published as the book *A Brief Tour of Human Consciousness*. Among Ramachandran's many honors are honorary life membership of the Royal Institution in Great Britain, and fellowships of All Souls College, Oxford and at Stanford University. In 1995 he was invited to give the "Decade of the Brain" lecture at the silver jubilee meeting of the Society for Neuroscience.

Ramachandran has always been attracted to natural anomalies that violate common sense, and in his early work this led him to focus on vision and visual illusions. Such illusions, he has said, are like magic, and the joy of science is to find an explanation for that magic. Later on Ramachandran turned his attention to behavioral neurology and the study of patients with seemingly mysterious conditions. These include "phantom limb syndrome," in which sensations are still felt in a missing limb; anosognosia, in which patients with problems such as paralysis deny that there is anything wrong with them; and Capgras syndrome, in which patients believe their loved ones have been replaced by imposters. Ramachandran is also credited with reigniting research interest in synaesthesia (see pages 24–25), and lately he has turned his attention to the search for universals in art, and to studying autism.

Phantom Limb Syndrome

Ramachandran was not the first person to document phantom limb syndrome, but his methods for studying the condition provide a good example of his Sherlock Holmes approach to science. For example, by using a pool cue to touch different parts of the body of a patient with phantom limb syndrome, Ramachandran was among the first to demonstrate the massive reorganization that is possible in the brain's sensory map of the body. When the patient was touched on his face, he reported experiencing a sensation in his missing hand. This sounds bizarre, but it turns out that the brain's representations of the face and hand are next to each other. In the absence of feedback from the hand, the tissue representing the patient's face had invaded the now redundant tissue that previously served his missing hand.

Ramachandran's playful attitude has also led him to propose one of the few ways that exist to help people experiencing phantom limb pain. Such pain can come about if, for example, the patient has the sensation that their missing hand is clenched uncomfortably tight. Inspired by findings showing how visual input can overrule other sensory information (as we saw with the rubber hand illusion on page 19), Ramachandran devised a box with a mirror in the middle of it, perpendicular to the patient. If a patient inserts their healthy hand on one side of the mirror and places their damaged limb on the other side, the reflection in the mirror gives the impression that their missing hand has been resurrected. The patient can then uncurl the fingers of their healthy hand, so giving the appearance in the mirror that the fingers of their missing hand are also uncurling, in some cases leading to the alleviation of their phantom pain.

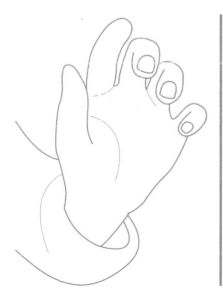 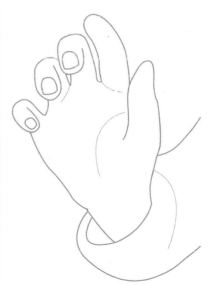

Perception and Action

THE PROBLEM:

You are the manager at a city library where there has been a spate of accidents on the steep stone steps leading up to the entrance. Local counsellors are anxious that it is just a matter of time until someone sues, and they've instructed you to do something to stop so many people tripping on the steps. It's a historic building and budgets are tight, so installing an escalator, ramps, or banisters isn't possible. You need to come up with a cheap and elegant solution.

THE METHOD:

Rather than making a radical alteration to the infrastructure of the building, you can use the psychology of perception to alter the way that people handle the hazard of the steps.

Although it feels as though we see the world as it really is, the perceptual system depends on various short-cuts and assumptions when processing incoming sensory information. These perceptual processes can be exploited or "hacked" by designers, thereby changing how people see the environment. If you alter people's perceptions, psychologists have demonstrated that you inevitably influence how they behave.

Take the example of Lake Shore Drive along the coast of Lake Michigan in Chicago, part of which features a series of tricky s-bends. Conventional signs telling drivers to slow down were largely ignored and the bendy, scenic stretch of road became an accident blackspot.

In 2006 the city tried a new approach and painted a series of horizontal lines across the road (perpendicular to oncoming cars). The spacing between the lines is gradually reduced, which gives drivers the impression that they are speeding up, thus encouraging them to take their foot off the gas. In the six months following the introduction of the lines, the number of crashes fell by 36 percent compared with the 6 months before the lines were drawn.

THE SOLUTION:

You can use a similar approach to encourage people to take more care on your library steps. In 2009, a team of British researchers led by David Elliott at the University of Bradford showed how a simple design intervention can change the way people perceive the height of steps, with consequences for how they step onto them.

Elliott's team painted horizontal stripes on the leading face of one step. On another step of identical height they painted vertical stripes. They first asked a group of volunteers to estimate the height of the steps. On average, the step with the vertical stripes was judged to be 5 mm higher. The crucial test, though, was whether people would act differently based on that illusion.

Next, the researchers filmed their volunteers stepping onto the steps and the important finding was that they lifted their foot higher when stepping onto the step with vertical stripes, as if it really were higher. This is significant because the majority of falls on steps are caused by people clipping the top of the step with their foot.

To help reduce the number of falls on the steps to your library you could try imitating the intervention used in this study. By painting vertical stripes (in tasteful colours) on the leading face of the steps, you will make them appear higher and thereby encourage visitors to lift their feet higher onto the steps as they climb up to the entrance.

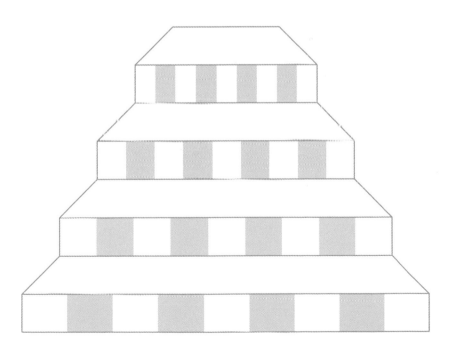

Memory

Without memory we have no identity. We depend
on it to remember who we are, where we've been,
and to recognize the people who matter most to us.
Contrary to the popular belief that memory is like a
video recorder, we'll learn—through exercises and
accounts of psychology studies—that it's actually a
highly creative, fallible process.

THE SEA SLUG

In many ways, memory is what makes us human. It provides our sense of identity, allows us to recognize the people we love, and to develop skills and learn about the world. Without memory, we'd be stuck in a Groundhog Day loop of endless re-enactment. So why, when memory is so central to what it means to be human, does this chapter begin with a discussion of the sea slug?

Well, for science to get a real grip on what memory is, it's been important to strip the concept down to its bare bones, to ask: What is memory in its most basic form? This has led to the realization that even relatively basic organisms, like slugs, show behavior that is indicative of learning. And learning, of course, depends on memory, or at least a memory-like capacity.

So the sea slug has allowed scientists to study some of the most rudimentary forms of memory. Still, you might fairly ask: why the sea slug rather than some other organism of similar complexity? The sea slug is also appealing to memory researchers because it has relatively few nerve cells—less than a million—many of which are quite large. In fact, some of the slug's nerve cells are up to a millimeter in diameter, in contrast to your own brain cells, which can be a hundred times narrower than that. Finally, the sea slug has easily identifiable nerve cells that can be studied in one individual creature, and then the same cell found and studied in another.

Habituation

Imagine you've bought a shiny new mobile phone which keeps beeping every hour and you don't know how to stop it. At first the hourly chime is annoying, but gradually you become so used to it happening that you barely notice it any more—in other words you habituate to it. This is one of the forms of learning shown by the sea slug and studied by the Nobel prize-winning scientist and memory pioneer Eric Kandel.

If you spray one of the sea slug's body parts, such as its gill, with sea water, it will withdraw the affected area from danger. But if you keep spraying, the slug will no longer show this withdrawal response because it will habituate to the sensation in the same way that you're no longer bothered by your phone's hourly chime. This kind of learning had been observed in other animals before, but only from the outside. Kandel looked under the hood. He studied in close detail the sensory neuron responsible for detecting the water spray, and the motor neuron that initiated the withdrawal response, to find out what was going on when the slug learned not to bother responding any longer.

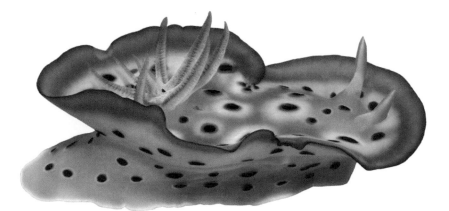

Communicating Cells

He found first that the sensory neuron still responds to the repeated stimulation. By directly activating the motor neuron, he was further able to show that muscle fatigue was playing no part in the habituation process. This meant something must be going on in between—most likely related to the way nerve cells communicate with each other through the release of brain chemicals (neurotransmitters). Indeed, experiments suggested that habituation led to a reduced amount of neurotransmitter being released by the sensory neuron. Crucially, this ability for experience to change communication between nerve cells is thought to underlie our own ability to lay down new memories.

Sensitization

You're sitting quietly reading when the smoke alarm goes off, almost causing you to hit the ceiling. There's no danger, it was only your friend burning toast in the kitchen. But knowing this doesn't stop you from feeling all jittery for the next few minutes, so that any unexpected noise has you on the edge of your seat. This ability for a powerful stimulus to put all our senses on edge is known as sensitization, and is another basic form of learning that Kandel studied in the sea slug. In this case, a noxious stimulus applied anywhere on the slug's body leaves its withdrawal response hyper-responsive for a length of time that depends on the strength of the earlier shock. Kandel's studies showed that whereas habituation is based on the sensory neuron releasing less neurotransmitter, sensitization seems to be caused by an "interneuron" affecting a given sensory neuron in such a way that it releases more neurotransmitter, thus leading to a heightened recoil response.

HOW MUCH CAN WE REMEMBER

With some estimates suggesting that the human cortex contains upward of 10 billion neurons and each neuron making connections with 100,000 other neurons, there probably isn't any meaningful limit to how much information we can store away. Of course, whether or not we can recall that information when we want it is a whole other question.

However, there is a kind of memory, known as short-term or "working" memory, which certainly does have limits and is more amenable to experimental measurement than long-term memory. Short-term memory is like your brain's desktop—it's what you use for holding information in mind for some purpose, such as when memorizing a telephone number before making a call.

TEST YOUR FRIENDS' SHORT-TERM MEMORY CAPACITY

A simple way to test working memory capacity is to read out a string of numbers of increasing length to your friends and see at what point they lose the ability to say the numbers back to you in the correct order. This is known as a digit-span task.

For example, start with just two numbers (4, 8) and wait for your friend to say them back. Then give them three to recall (2, 5, 9) and keep going like that all the way up to... let's say a string of ten numbers. Of course you can get a friend to test you in the same fashion. What you'll probably find is that you and your friends are able to recall somewhere between five and nine numbers in the correct order. This is a robust finding in psychology research and was most famously discussed by George Miller in his seminal paper "The Magical Number Seven, Plus or Minus Two."

CHUNKING

However, things aren't quite so simple as they seem because this limit of seven, plus or minus two, applies to the number of meaningful chunks of information you're trying to recall, rather than the raw information. For example, we can recall approximately seven names, even though those names are made up of many more letters. You can test this out using the box below:

B	A	U	A	T
S	H	S	S	S
I	K	S	I	A
H	O	I	S	L
T	O	S	E	B

Try reading out the letters to a friend, starting from the bottom left-hand corner and working up each column in turn, beginning with just two letters at a time, then three at a time, and so on as you did earlier with numbers. At first, you might find your friend's memory is limited to around seven letters, as before. But if your friend is particularly shrewd they may start to recognize that the letters spell out a message which, once decoded, will make it easy for them to recall all 25 letters. That's because once the message is decoded, the letters can then be understood as forming seven meaningful chunks.

Disrupting Short-Term Memory

A vast amount of evidence points to the idea that we hold items in short-term memory by verbally rehearsing them silently in our mind—just think of how you say an unfamiliar phone number over and over to yourself before dialing. One way you can test out this idea is by repeating the earlier digit-span tests on your friend—but this time get them to repeat an unrelated word out loud ("the," "the," "the") as they perform the task. You should find their memory performance suffers, presumably because the inner rehearsal process of their short-term memory has been compromised by their vocal utterances.

A related way to disrupt short-term memory is via a phenomenon known as

the "irrelevant sound effect." To observe this in action, you can once again test a friend on the digit-span task, but this time do it within earshot of some irrelevant speech—a talk radio station should do the trick. In fact, it doesn't even have to be speech—the disruption is caused by any kind of sound that is made up of distinct chunks, such as staccato music with clear gaps between the notes. Again, as with their repetition of the word "the," you should find your friend's performance is compromised. There's still some controversy over how this interference occurs, but it's likely it also disrupts the silent rehearsal of items to be remembered.

WAYS OF FORGETTING

In classic amnesia, the patient will probably know their name, have a reasonable sense of their life story, and will even be able to recall things, such as a phone number, over very short time periods. So far, so good, but ask them where they were yesterday or what they had for breakfast and they will look at you blankly. This is known as a deficit in episodic memory or anterograde amnesia, and reflects an inability to lay down new long-lasting memories.

This kind of amnesia can have many causes, from stroke, to a condition known as Korsakoff's syndrome, which is seen in alcoholics who have been eating so poorly that they are left with a thiamine deficiency. A hit to the head—for example in a car crash—can also lead to amnesia. When this happens the patient will usually also suffer a loss of memory for events leading up to the crash, which is called retrograde amnesia. This period can be many years long, but often the memories will gradually return, beginning with the earliest, until a point near the moment of the crash, which will remain lost for ever.

Tales of Forgetfulness

Perhaps the most compelling fictional portrayal of what it must be like to suffer from anterograde amnesia is to be found in the film *Momento*, starring Guy Pierce. The lead character develops memory problems after a blow to his head, and in his search for his wife's killer, resorts to obsessive compensatory strategies, even tattooing key clues to the case on his body.

The most famous real-life amnesic is probably a patient known as H.M. He was an epilepsy sufferer whose seizures grew so bad that in the 1950s surgeons decided to remove a sea-horse shaped region called the hippocampus from both sides of his brain. Unfortunately, the surgeons at the time didn't realize the vital role played by the hippocampus, and after his operation H.M.'s memory was severely impaired, even though his personality and overall IQ remained relatively unaffected. However, one form of memory that remained intact in H.M., which is typical of amnesics, was his implicit memory. This meant he was able to learn new skills, such as puzzles or mazes, even though he would have no recollection of ever having seen them before.

A particularly famous anecdote of how implicit memory can remain intact in amnesics was told by the Swiss psychologist Édouard Claparède. One day Claparède concealed a pin in his palm before shaking hands with an amnesic patient. The next day the same patient refused to take his hand, though she couldn't explain why.

THE CHAMELEON MAN

In the cases we've discussed so far, the amnesic patients have generally retained their sense of who they are. However, more rarely there are reports of patients who appear to have lost their identity.

In 2007, psychologists reported the real-life case of A.D., a 65-year-old whose identity appeared to be dependent on the environment he was in. His strange behavior began after a heart attack caused him to suffer damage to the fronto-temporal region of his brain. When he was with doctors, A.D. assumed the role of a doctor. When with psychologists he acted as though he were a psychologist, and when he was at the solicitors… that's right, he claimed to be a solicitor. But apparently, A.D. didn't just say "I am a doctor" or "I am a psychologist;" he actually acted out the roles and provided plausible stories for how he came to be the character he believed he was.

To test just how malleable A.D.'s sense of identity was, Giovannina Conchiglia and colleagues used actors to contrive different scenarios. For example, at a bar, an actor asked A.D. for a cocktail, prompting him to immediately adopt the role of bar-tender, claiming that he was on probation and hoping to gain a permanent position. In a hospital kitchen for just 40 minutes, A.D. claimed the role of head chef, saying he was responsible for the special meals required by diabetic patients.

A.D. maintained these assumed roles until the situation changed. The psychologists studying him said his condition was a mixture of a disinhibition syndrome—similar to utilization behavior, in which patients can't help themselves from using any objects or food in the vicinity—anterograde amnesia, and anosognosia, which is a lack of insight into one's disabilities or strange behavior.

However, there were limits to the roles A.D. would take on. For example, he didn't adopt the role of laundry worker at the hospital laundry, perhaps because it was rather beneath his real-life career as a politician!

AD = L
AD = M
AD = N
AD = O
AD = P
AD = Q
AD = R

AD = S
AD = T
AD = U
AD = V
AD = W
AD = X
AD = Y

FORGETTING FACES

Most of us are remarkable face experts. Usually, all it takes is for us to meet someone once and their face seems to become embedded into our memory banks. We can even identify people from strange angles and in the most unhelpful lighting. However, there are some people for whom this expertise is lacking—they can't even recognize photographs of themselves. Their face blindness is known technically as prosopagnosia, from the Greek for prosopo meaning face, and *agnosia*, meaning without knowledge.

Historically, face blindness was considered to be extremely rare, resulting from brain damage caused by stroke or an accident. Probably the most famous neurological case was reported by Oliver Sacks in his book *The Man Who Mistook His Wife for a Hat*. But in the last few years, researchers have realized that many people are actually born with the condition. For example, from a web survey of 1600 people, psychologist Bradley Duchaine and colleagues found that around 2 percent of people have some degree of face blindness. Experts think it's probably gone under-reported because many people who grow up face-blind don't realize how unusual their deficit is.

Reasons for Forgetfulness

The fact that some people suffer face blindness after a specific part of their brain has been damaged has led some psychologists to suggest that we have a kind of dedicated "face processing" module. Supporting their argument is the finding that a specific area of the brain— the so-called fusiform face area or FFA—is activated particularly strongly when we look at people's faces.

However, other experts disagree. They believe that our impressive ability with faces is just one of many possible forms of expertise. Our ability to identify faces just happens to be particularly strong, they say, because we're exposed to people's faces every day of our lives. Supporting their argument is the fact that people who develop other forms of recognition expertise, such as the ability of bird watchers to distinguish between species, also show activation in the FFA, albeit to a lesser extent, when they look at birds.

IMPAIR YOUR FRIENDS' FACE RECOGNITION

For this experiment you need to get hold of photos of the faces of 28 strangers (not celebrities). You could try cutting them out of magazines or printing them off the internet. If you can, make sure the size of the photos is as similar as possible, and that only the face region is shown.

Now you need to test as many friends as possible. Taking each friend in turn, present 14 of the faces to them, one at a time, for about three seconds each. You'll need to mark these 14 faces on the back in some way, so that you can keep track of which faces you've shown and which you've kept behind.

For half your friends, after they've seen these 14 faces, get them to read for five minutes. For the other half, get them to attempt a cryptic crossword for the same length of time—this is a task that's been found to disrupt people's memory for faces.

Now for the second stage. Mix up the original 14 faces with the remainder you didn't use before, and then present all 28 of them, one at a time, to your friends. Their task is to say in each case whether the face was one of the ones shown to them earlier or not. During this second stage, make sure you keep a score of your friends' accuracy, and you should also leave about 30 seconds between the presentation of each of the faces, during which time your friends must continue with their reading or cryptic crossword efforts.

When you tally up the scores, you'll hopefully find that the scores of the friends whom did the cryptic crossword average out as significantly less accurate than the friends who you asked to read. If you

managed all this, then you will have replicated a study published by Cardiff-based psychologist Michael Lewis in the journal *Perception*.

According to his report, Lewis isn't sure why doing cryptic crosswords has this effect on face recognition, but he thinks a clue could come from the fact that so-called Navon stimuli also have this interfering effect. Navon stimuli are images in which a large letter or symbol is composed of many tiny repeats of a different letter or symbol. What cryptic crosswords and Navon stimuli may have in common is that they involve suppressing obvious, irrelevant information, which presumably has some kind of detrimental effect on the way our brains process faces. Incidentally, Lewis also tested participants with simple crosswords and Sudoku puzzles, but they didn't have the same face-blinding effect.

ERASING BAD MEMORIES

Memories of days like 9/11 or even our first day at work, which take place under particularly emotional or stressful circumstances, tend to become etched into our brains and are known as "flash-bulb memories." This process makes sense from an evolutionary point of view—if we've been endangered or something happens that is of profound importance to our lives, it should help our future survival if we remember it well. The trouble is, the same process means that some people are unable to forget experiences that they'd rather leave behind.

The unwanted reliving of previous life-threatening experiences, in the form of flash-backs and nightmares, is today known as post-traumatic stress disorder (PTSD), which is also covered on pages 140–41. By some estimates, 49 percent of rape victims experience PTSD and around 30 percent of bomb victims. During World War I, the same condition was referred to as shell shock, and descriptions of trauma-like symptoms in fact date back to ancient Egyptian times.

Memory Blockers

Particularly threatening situations activate an almond-shaped structure found deep in the brain called the amygdala. This in turn leads to a rush of adrenaline and noradrenaline, which is thought to affect the processing of the sea-horse shaped hippocampus—a key brain area involved in human memory. The consequence is that we form a particularly long-lasting record of what happened, thus explaining the persistence of traumatic memories.

Greater understanding of these processes has prompted scientists to wonder if it might be possible to disrupt the forming of unpleasant memories, and so help prevent PTSD. Early findings seem to offer some hope. Psychiatrist Guillaume Vaiva and colleagues tested the effect of propranolol, a beta blocker that is taken by some cardiac patients. Propranolol binds to the same cell-surface receptors as adrenaline and noradrenaline. The theory is that it should be able to disrupt the formation of long-lasting traumatic memories by blocking the role played by these neurotransmitters.

Vaiva's team struck an agreement with the emergency department of the Douai and Lille Hospitals in France, such that patients arriving intact but shocked, from car crashes or physical assault, were given the option to take propranolol three times daily for the next seven days. Eleven patients agreed to this, while eight others declined to take propranolol but agreed to participate in the study. There was no difference in the severity of the trauma experienced by the two groups of patients, but when a psychiatrist assessed them two months later, he found PTSD symptoms were far lower in the group who took propranolol.

Propranolol could even help reduce the impact of traumatic memories formed years, even decades, ago. Research on mice has shown that when stressful memories are recalled there is a brief period during which they are vulnerable to unlearning or adjustment, even if they were originally laid down a long time ago. Inspired by this observation, in 2007 American psychiatrist Roger Pitman investigated what would happen if patients with PTSD were given propranolol after recalling their traumatic memories, even though these memories were for events that had happened many years ago. A week later, when the patients listened to a recorded account of their traumatic experience, the patients previously given propranolol suffered far less stress than those given a placebo.

Another possible approach to erasing traumatic memories is to target the brain hormone cortisol. The intensive care doctor Gustav Schelling noticed that PTSD is less common in septic shock patients who are given the immunosuppressant hydrocortisone, which is a synthetic form of cortisol. He and his colleagues have since tested the effect of giving hydrocortisone to 14 patients about to undergo cardiac surgery. Such patients often experience a great deal of post-operative stress, and in some cases PTSD. However, hydrocortisone significantly decreased these stress-related symptoms as compared with another group of patients given a placebo. Of course, larger-scale trials of all these effects are needed, but the results are certainly promising.

Ethical Concerns

Most experts agree that it is just a matter of time before a reliable method of erasing unwanted memories is developed, but because of the ethical implications, not everyone believes this is good news. For example, what if the same techniques are used to wipe the memories of witnesses to crimes? Or what will happen to the guiding influence of emotions like guilt, if a clear conscience is only a tablet away?

TEN WAYS TO BOOST YOUR MEMORY

Learn Mnemonics

When Eleanor Maguire and colleagues scanned the brains of ten world memory champions in 2003, they didn't find anything unusual about their brain structure or general IQ. However, during a memory task, the researchers found that brain areas related to movement and navigation were activated in the champs' brains, but not in the brains of ordinary folk. This probably reflects the way the champs used a mnemonic strategy called the "method of loci," which involves imagining items to be remembered (such as cards or numbers) as meaningful objects or people placed in various positions along a familiar route or journey.

Do Puzzles

The old adage "Use it or lose it" really does seem to be true when it comes to brain power. A study by Robert Wilson and colleagues of 801 nuns, priests, and monks over five years found that those who kept themselves busy with crosswords and games were less likely to develop Alzheimer's Disease.

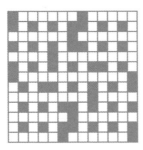

Get Mobile

Mobile phones get a lot of bad press, with fears over cancer and the dangers of chatting while driving. But in 2006, Australian psychologist Vanessa Keetley found that 30 minutes with a mobile phone clipped to the side of the head led participants to perform better at a test of short-term memory. The researchers said the phones may have altered blood flow in the dorsolateral prefrontal cortex, an area involved in working memory. Not one to try at home until more research is conducted.

Wiggle Your Eyes

It sounds daft, but in 2007 Andrew Parker and Neil Dagnall reported that participants who wiggled their eyes from left to right after learning a list of words, subsequently remembered more of the words than participants who stared straight ahead or who wiggled their eyes up and down. The psychologists said moving the eyes from side to side can help the two brain hemispheres communicate with each other.

Summarize and Integrate

Summarizing the main points of what you've learned, and thinking deeply about how they relate to what you already knew and to your own experiences, leads to longer-lasting memories—a process known as "knowledge integration." One way to do this is to try to explain to your friends and family what you've just learned.

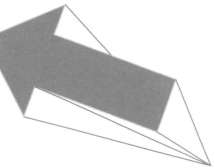

Sleep On It

A good night's sleep after learning is important if you want to consolidate your memories, but so too is having a solid snooze before you start studying. In 2007, Matthew Walker and colleagues found that sleep-deprived participants remembered 19 percent fewer pictures relative to controls who'd slept well. Brain scans showed less activity in the hippocampus of the sleep-deprived, a brain area responsible for laying down new memories.

Smart Drugs

Drugs like Modafinil—officially a treatment for narcolepsy—are already being hailed as "cognitive enhancers" for their beneficial effects on mental performance, including memory. But elsewhere concerns have been raised about the safety and ethics of using drugs in this way. For example, in 2007, psychologists Barbara Sahakian and Sharon Morein-Zamir wrote that when it comes to cognitive enhancers, proper regulation needs to catch up with the science.

Electrify Your Brain

When Canadian surgeons attempted to curtail the appetite of a dangerously obese man by stimulating an area deep in his brain called the hypothalamus, they were startled when he started recalling memories from decades earlier. Later tests showed that zapping the same area boosted his memory performance, and trials are now under way with Alzheimer's sufferers.

Eat Well

Especially when it comes to breakfast. Nutritionist Barbara Stewart reported in 2003 that children, especially girls, performed better on tests of attention and memory when they'd had beans on toast for breakfast, rather than just toast. Also, eat lots of fish—the "brain food" of choice. The fatty acids found in fish help prevent your brain from clogging up with trans-fats.

Pace out Your Studies

Cramming doesn't work. The secret to remembering material in the long term is to review what you've studied periodically. Psychologists Doug Rohrer and Harold Pashler have conducted experiments showing that the optimum time after which you should review previously learned material is 10 to 30 percent of the total time for which you want to remember it. So if you've working toward an exam that's due in ten days time, don't keep over-learning what you've studied; instead you're better off leaving the material and reviewing it a day later. If the exam is six months later, review the material after a month.

FEELING ALL NOSTALGIC

Ah, I remember it like it was only yesterday: My wife and I walking together along the Champs Élysées, the sun shining, birds singing away, traffic screeching past—those were the days. Sorry, I've come over all nostalgic. We all do from time to time, but what is nostalgia and what purpose does it serve?

Nostalgia, from the Greek, means literally a return (nostos) of pain (algos), and indeed, doctors in the seventeenth and eighteenth centuries tended to think of nostalgia as a form of melancholy or even a neurological disorder. But today psychologists have a quite different view. Their experiments are showing that nostalgia can rescue us from misery when we're feeling down and lend meaning to our lives at times of existential crisis.

In a study by Tim Wildschut and colleagues, several dozen university students completed a measure of their loneliness, but with a twist. Afterward they were given false feedback, so that half of them were told they were much lonelier than the average student, and the other half were told they were much less lonely. To reinforce the false feedback, the students were then asked to write about why they had scored the way they had.

After all this, the students completed a measure of nostalgia with some of the items being similar to those in the scale shown below. It turned out that the students who were tricked into believing they were lonely subsequently scored much higher on the nostalgia scale, supporting the psychologists' prediction that one role played by nostalgia is to comfort us from loneliness. Consistent with this, other research has shown that nostalgic thoughts often seem to feature other people.

Thoughts of Death

In another study, Clay Routledge and colleagues asked students to think about what will happen to their bodies when they die. Later they were asked to complete ambiguous word fragments like COFF--. As expected, thinking about death made morbid thoughts more accessible to the students' minds, as evinced by their tendency to come up with morbid word endings (such as COFFIN rather than COFFEE). Crucially, however, this effect was much reduced among the students who earlier tests had shown were more prone to nostalgia, supporting the psychologists' belief that another function served by nostalgia is to protect us from existential angst.

HOW NOSTALGIC ARE YOU

These are the kinds of questions psychologists have used in their studies of nostalgia:

1. I miss the way things were.
2. I sometimes reflect on bad things that have happened to me.
3. Overall there are more good things in my past than bad things.
4. I sometimes find myself thinking of the things I've missed out on in life.
5. Memories of happy times often pop into my mind.
6. I don't like thinking about the past because of bad things that have happened.
7. I sometimes reminisce fondly about my childhood.
8. I often think about holidays I've been on.

What's Your Earliest Memory?

If you're like most people, you won't be able to recall any memories from before you were about three and a half to four years old. Any memories from before this time appear to be lost forever, thanks to what psychologists call "infantile amnesia." This gap in our memories is a bit of a mystery because two- and three-year-olds gladly talk about events from a year or so earlier in their lives, showing that memories from our very earliest years were at some point laid down in verbally accessible long-term memory.

In 2005 psychologist Carole Peterson and colleagues found that children younger than ten had earlier first memories (from when they were about three) than older children, but that after ten and up to adulthood there was no difference in the time of earliest memories, regardless of increasing age. The researchers said they had no idea what happens to our earlier memories when we pass the age of ten.

SCORING

Each time you answer "yes," a point is scored. Subtract any points for items 2, 4, and 6 from the total.

1 point or less: *Don't Look Back in Anger*—you're not at all nostalgic.

2-3 points: *Happy Days*—you're fairly nostalgic.

4-5 points: *Yesterday All My Troubles Seemed So Far Away*—you're always dreaming fondly of the past.

Elizabeth Loftus and false memories

"The truly horrifying idea is that what we think we know, what we believe with all our hearts, is not necessarily the truth."
Loftus speaking to *Psychology Today* magazine, 1996.

Elizabeth Loftus (née Fishman) has studied memory for nearly 40 years and is best known for her work showing the malleability of memory and the suggestibility of eye witnesses. In the process she has received death threats and the highest awards obtainable in psychology, including in 2005 the Grawemeyer Award for Psychology, worth a cool U.S.$200,000. In 2002, Loftus was listed as one of the top 100 most influential psychologists of the twentieth century by the *Review of General Psychology*—the highest-ranked woman on the list.

Loftus began her career by studying the way people classify animals and fruit, but soon decided she wanted her research to be more

socially relevant. In this regard she couldn't have been more successful, having since consulted and testified in hundreds of criminal trials, including the case of Michael Jackson, the Bosnian War trials in the Hague, and the 2006 trial of Scooter Libby. Today Loftus is a distinguished professor at the University of California, Irvine, having previously held professorships at the University of Washington, Seattle, where she taught for 29 years.

Some of Loftus's most compelling research has shown how easy it is to implant false memories in people's minds. For example, in one of her earliest studies, she and colleagues gave adult participants false feedback from relatives suggesting, alongside other truthful accounts, that they had had the experience of getting lost in a shopping mall as a child. The participants were asked to provide additional details of the incident if they could. A couple of weeks later, the participants were again asked about the shopping mall incident, by which time many of them claimed to have memories of this fictitious event, in some cases even embellishing it with their own details.

Recovered Memory

In a more recent version of the study, Loftus and colleagues were able to put hundreds of undergraduate students off strawberry ice cream. All it took was false feedback from a computer program telling them about "that time" they were made sick by strawberry ice cream as a child.

Loftus's research in this field has proved so controversial because of the claims of some therapists that they can help patients recover long-repressed memories of abuse—so-called

MANIPULATE YOUR FRIEND'S MEMORIES

First devise a list of between twenty and forty plausible life events that a person might have experienced as a child. Examples could include: "got into trouble for talking in class," "went to meet Santa Claus at a shopping mall," "had your tooth extracted at the dentist," and so on. Within that list, insert the following critical items: "broke a window with your hand," "had a lifeguard pull you out of the water," "got in trouble for calling 911."

Now find a willing friend and invite them to fill out this form, indicating which experiences they had as a child, and for each item, get them to say how confident they are that they really had that experience. Afterward, ask them to use their imagination and spend four minutes

thinking and writing about the four critical incidents, even if they're pretty sure they hadn't experienced them.

Then leave the task for two weeks, and don't even mention it during that time. Afterward, get your friend to complete the life-event list again, including rating their confidence in their memories for each item. If the experiment has worked, you will find this time around that your friends' confidence in their memory for the critical incidents has increased. If this happens, you will have replicated an experiment by Charles Manning, a Ph.D. student of Elizabeth Loftus, showing how easy it is for us to confuse imagined events with real memories—part of the process that can lead to the generation of false memories.

"recovered memories." Loftus's work suggests that in many cases such memories are likely to be false. Loftus has also shown how easy it is for trial witnesses to be influenced. Indeed, even subtle changes to the way people are asked

questions can bias their answers. For example, ask a witness how fast they think two cars were going when they "smashed" into each other, and they're likely to give you a faster estimate than if asked about the time the cars "hit" each other.

Memory

THE PROBLEM:

You're at a job interview and already the pressure is making you feel a little hot under the collar. All of sudden your stern-faced inquisitor throws you a curve ball: "Can you name the last three presidents of the United States?" That's easy, you think to yourself as you begin the list ... Obama, Bush ... but then, to your horror, your mind goes completely blank. The interviewer raises a condescending eyebrow as the room begins to close in around you. How can you salvage the situation?

THE METHOD:

Temporarily forgetting material we know we know is an all too common occurrence. Technically speaking, one cause is what's known as interference. As you reached for the name of the final relevant president, perhaps your mind filled with the names of lots of other presidents–the wrong ones. If they became activated too strongly in your mind, this would have had the effect of crowding out the correct answer.

This kind of memory problem can happen to the best of us. In 2011, the Republican presidential candidate Rick Perry was asked in a national TV debate to name the three government departments that it was his policy to abolish. After naming the first two (commerce and education), he stumbled on the third. In front of an audience of millions he was humiliated by his inability to articulate his own policy. The more the debate chair pressed him, the more Perry squirmed as the correct answer, which he knew he knew, continued to evade him. He made the situation worse by repeating the two departments he could think of, further suppressing his chances of recalling the final department.

The way memorized information competes for our attention was also demonstrated by a classic study in the 1960s. Participants given the names of half the US states found it more difficult to name the remaining half, as compared with another group of participants who were tasked with naming all 50 without any help. It's as if the name of the first 25 states captured the first group's attention, interfering with their ability to recall the remaining states.

THE SOLUTION:

How can these insights help you in the interview room? Two further psychological observations are worth highlighting. When we try too hard to stop thinking about something, it usually backfires, an effect that psychologists call an "ironic rebound." Similarly, once our mind is on the wrong track, the harder we try to find the right answer, the more we can end up digging ourselves into a rut. This means you need to relax, stop trying too hard to reach for the answer (in the wrong place), and stop trying too hard to not think of all the wrong answers that keep entering your mind.

Some of these principles were demonstrated in a 2008 study that looked at tip-of-the-tongue states—when the word you want remains tantalisingly out of mental reach. Amy Warriner and Karin Humphreys provoked people into these states by asking them to name obscure objects like the abacus. The longer they left a participant in a tip-of-the-tongue state before telling them the correct answer, the

more likely that person was to experience the frustrating state again when prompted for the word two days later. It's as if more time spent looking in the wrong place on day one had established a mental habit, making the mishap more likely to repeat.

At your interview, on realizing that you know the correct answer, but that it is proving elusive, you should request politely but assertively that you would like to move onto the next question. Reassure the interviewer that you will provide the answer in due course. Changing your mental focus to a new question will allow the relevant items in your memory to settle back to their baseline activity levels. And perhaps most important, taking a break will stop you travelling deeper down the wrong corridor of your mind.

After a few moments talking about something completely different, you'll likely find that the word "Clinton" pops into your head. Phew! Now when the interviewer returns to the president question, you can take pleasure in wiping that patronizing look off his face.

3

Cognition

Early in the twentieth century, a branch of psychology known as behaviorism argued that we should only study outwardly observable behavior, leaving the workings of the mind as a black box. That all changed from the 1950s onwards with the cognitive revolution, as psychologists focused ever more on the internal processes of the mind. This chapter is about those mental functions, including language, intelligence, decision making, and number crunching.

FIVE FLAWS IN YOUR THINKING

We like to think of ourselves as rational beings, but in fact we're subject to numerous biases of egotism, self-deception, and wonky thinking. Here are five examples:

Stranger To Yourself

From unused gym memberships to broken promises to visit relatives, we're always committing ourselves to ventures that seem somehow less appealing once they arrive. It's almost as though our current selves, who make the arrangements, think our future selves are going to be so much more dedicated and patient. However, there is a positive side to this. Researchers have shown that we tend to underestimate our capacity to deal with unfortunate future events. When healthy people are asked to imagine the impact of a potential chronic illness on their mood, they see its likely effect as devastating. Yet when psychologists measured the mood of patients with end-state renal disease, requiring hemodialysis three times per week, it turned out they were just as happy as a group of healthy participants.

Unjustified Optimism

We underestimate our ability to cope with adverse events, but paradoxically we're also overly optimistic in that we think bad things are far more likely to happen to other people. A library's worth of studies have revealed the following anomalies: Students think they are less likely than average to suffer in their lifetime from a drink problem or early heart attack, or get fired from a job; smokers think they are less vulnerable than most to the ill effects of cigarettes; newlyweds accurately guess divorce rates, but think their marriage will thrive; young people think they're less likely than average to fall pregnant or contract HIV. The bias extends to dating and shopping. Men tend to interpret a smile from a woman as a sign that she is interested in them. Credit card users choose cards with high interest rates and a low annual fee because they fail to anticipate the debt they are going to accumulate.

You're More Generous to an Individual than the Needy Masses

No doubt you consider yourself a fair person. And yet, if you're like the rest of us, a story of a single suffering individual pulls on your heart strings far more forcefully than newspaper reports of a disaster affecting thousands. Think of how the world was gripped by the disappearance of the British girl Madeleine McCann in Portugal, while elsewhere in the world many thousands of unidentified children go missing or are starved or killed every day. Unfortunately, when psychologist Deborah Small tested what would happen to participants if they were educated about this bias, she found the discrepancy disappeared, not because participants donated more to the millions of starving people in Africa, but because they chose to give less to a single seven-year-old girl whose plight they'd read about.

The "Power of One"

There's something about one unit or portion that we find appealing, a bias that Andrew Geier and colleagues at the University of Pennsylvania believe could underlie our irrational eating habits. In one study they left a bowl of M&M sweets in the hallway of an apartment building with a sign saying "Help Yourself." How many sweets did people take? It depended on the size of the spoon left in the bowl—with people eating more if the spoon was bigger. Similarly, measured by weight, significantly more pretzels were taken by passers-by when a complimentary bowl of 60 whole pretzels was left in an apartment building, compared with a bowl of 120 half-pretzels. The bias extends to other walks of life too.

As Quentin Tarantino discovered with his double feature *Grindhouse: Planet Terror/Death Proof*, people these days don't much like double-bills at the cinema, but they'll gladly sit through one long movie. Likewise, one fairground ride is usually enough, whether it lasts five minutes or half an hour.

You're Wooed by Simple Names

Economists have been trying to predict share price fluctuations for years without success. The mistake they've made is to assume that people choose which shares to invest in on the basis of rational decisions. They'd have had more joy if they'd appreciated the human tendency to favor easily processed information. Indeed, when Adam Alter and Daniel Oppenheimer at Princeton University analyzed real stock-market records, they found that, over a year, new shares in companies with fluent, easy-to-pronounce names like "Barnings Inc." tended to outperform shares in companies with awkward names such as "Aegeadux Inc."

ISSUES OF INTELLIGENCE

There are probably more definitions of intelligence than there are intelligence experts. In fact psychologists haven't even been able to agree on how many types of braininess there are.

Flavors of Intelligence

Early in the twentieth century, the ex-army officer and psychologist Charles Spearman proposed that there is really just one kind of intelligence, which he said explains why a person's performance on one form of intelligence test will predict their performance on a second. By contrast, the psychologist Joy Guilford argued there are a whopping 120 different types. Howard Gardner of Harvard University has pitched for something in between, believing that there are between seven and nine and a half forms of intelligence, including musical ability and kinaesthetic skills.

The Function of Intelligence

How can we discuss intelligence without agreement as to what it is, or whether it's a unitary concept? Despite the disagreements, most experts share the view that what we mean by intelligence is something to do with a person's capacity to

learn and adapt. If a person is perceived to be intelligent by their culture, this is another way of saying that they have the tools needed to thrive in it; and, all other things being equal, they should therefore succeed in that environment relative to someone judged to be unintelligent. It follows from this that any meaningful measure of intelligence should have some predictive value.

Looked at in this functional sense, rather than more philosophically, intelligence tests do indeed seem to be measuring something of value. Intelligence tests have been found to predict exam performance, work performance, and even mortality. Indeed, IQ tests predict work performance better than interviews, job references, and years in education. Intelligence-test performance also correlates with biological measures, such as brain size and reaction time, and to some extent it runs in families, lending further credence to the idea that something concrete and meaningful is being measured.

Are We Getting Cleverer?

Throughout the last century, each generation has tended to perform significantly better on tests of intelligence, suggesting that we are getting cleverer. The pattern, dubbed the "Flynn effect" after the eponymous Professor James Flynn of

1. Key is to lock, as hand is to ... which of the following: **(a)** door, **(b)** glove, **(c)** clock, **(d)** bolt, **(e)** safe, or **(f)** palm

2. Study the following series of numbers: 41, 27, 16, 8, ..., 1, and select the correct missing number from:
(a) 10, **(b)** 2, **(c)** 7, **(d)** 3, **(e)** 64

3. 420 people live in four villages. Half live in the largest village, with the remaining distributed equally among the three smaller villages. How many people live in each small village? 70

4. What is the capital of Australia?

5.

I	II	III
II	III	I
III	I	?

Select the missing icon from the following:
(a) II   **(d)** III
(b) II   **(e)** I
(c) IIII   **(f)** II

6. Canoe   Fish
Which one of the following has something in common with the above two, which it doesn't share with the others: **(a)** tractor, **(b)** dog, **(c)** skis, **(d)** submarine, **(e)** bicycle, **(f)** rabbit

the University of Otago in New Zealand, has been observed in every country that has long enough records.

However, Flynn has argued that these gains are not really a sign that we have grown more intelligent. Rather, modern life and scientific progress has changed our style of thinking. In particular, he says we tend to see the similarities between things, whereas our ancestors were more interested in what things are useful for.

For example, asked what a dog and a rabbit have in common, we'd recognize them both as mammals, whereas an ancestor would recognize only that you use a dog to hunt rabbits. This argument is borne out by a closer look at the parts of intelligence tests that we've collectively shown the greatest improvements on. We've shown huge gains on the "similarities" subscale of the Wechsler Intelligence Scale for Children, but only small gains on measures of verbal and general knowledge.

ANSWERS

1. b 2. 3 3. 70 4. Canberra 5. b 6. d

We've also shown gains on a type of test called Raven's Progressive Matrices, a highly visual test (containing items similar to 5, above). Again, Flynn suggests this improvement probably reflects the fact that, with the ubiquity of TVs and computers, modern life has become more visual and abstract. If we had really become more intelligent you'd expect to see similar improvements on tests targeting arithmetic skills, yet gains here have been virtually non-existent.

DISRUPTED COGNITION

Classic neuropsychologists made many of their most important discoveries by studying patients with damage to specific parts of their brains. If a patient presented with a complaint such as a short-term memory problem, and it was later revealed at autopsy that they had suffered localized brain damage, then this would suggest, though by no means prove, that the afflicted brain area was somehow involved in short-term memory. The psychologist could further tentatively conclude that the patient's preserved mental faculties were not dependent on the damaged brain area for their healthy functioning.

Compartmentalizing the Brain

Extending this line of reasoning, neuropsychologists have paid particular attention to cases where one patient has a deficit in one domain (say short-term memory) but not another (long-term memory), while a second patient has the reverse deficit—impaired long-term memory, but intact short-term memory. This is known as a double-dissociation and provides powerful evidence that the two faculties operate independently of each other. If the two patients also have differing patterns of brain damage, further strong inferences can be made about the neuroanatomical basis of the mental domains in question.

One of the most famous examples of this kind of approach to psychology comes from the work of the French surgeon Paul Broca and the German neurologist Carl Wernicke in the nineteenth century. Broca reported the case of a patient with localized damage to the rear part of his left frontal lobe, whose comprehension was intact, but who could only utter the syllable "tan," hence his nickname "Tan-tan." By contrast, Wernicke described a syndrome following damage to the temporal lobe, which left patients able to produce speech, but with their comprehension devastated, with the consequence that what they said was often garbled nonsense. Taken together, these observations show how the comprehension and production of speech are handled separately by the brain.

Don't Try This at Home

Today psychologists can mimic this approach by using a hand-held magnet to temporarily disrupt activity in a localized area of a volunteer's brain, so inducing a "virtual" lesion. The technique is known as "transcranial magnetic stimulation" (TMS) and was developed by Sheffield University researchers in the early 1980s as a way of overcoming the electrical resistance of the skull. Holding a pulsing magnet over a volunteer's head induces a rapidly changing magnetic field in the neural tissue beneath, thus altering the electrical communication between brain cells. Stimulation at low frequency generally inhibits brain activity, while higher frequencies increase brain activity in the affected region.

A key advantage of the technique is that if knocking out a given brain area results in some behavioral effect, researchers can then conclude confidently that the affected brain region is "necessary" for that behavioral function. By contrast, when brain scanning reveals that a given brain region is active during a particular behavioral task, researchers can only conclude that the activity and the function are correlated—they can't infer any causal relation between the two.

In recent years psychologists have even started using TMS in ways that go beyond the virtual lesion approach. For example, in 2005 Alessio Avenanti and colleagues stimulated the motor region of participants' brains, so that their hands twitched. Crucially, they found that the TMS induced less twitching when it was applied as the participants watched another person being injected in their hand, compared with watching that person injected in the foot, or watching a tomato being injected. What was going on? The finding suggests that when we watch someone else have a painful experience, our brains inhibit motor activity in the corresponding part of our own body, just as would happen if we were experiencing the pain ourselves. Avenanti's experiment has added to the growing evidence showing that we empathize with other people's pain by simulating their experiences in our own brains.

SO WHAT WAS PHRENOLOGY

The phrenologists of the eighteenth and nineteenth centuries shared with more modern thinking the view that the mind is rooted in the brain. However, whereas modern-day psychologists consider different mental processes to be carried out by localized brain areas, the phrenologists wrongly argued that entire personality traits were somehow localized to a certain brain area, and that they could be read via bumps on the skull. At the height of its popularity, phrenology boasted many societies around the world dedicated to its study. Today, some sceptical commentators believe the localization of function or "blobs on the brain" approach to psychology has gone too far, and accuse their brain-imaging colleagues of being like modern-day phrenologists.

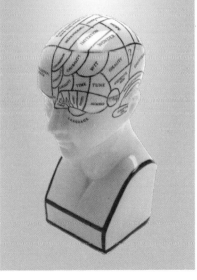

SPEAKING OF THOUGHTS

Can we think about things for which we lack the relevant words? Writing in the first half of the twentieth century, the linguist Edward Sapir and his student Benjamin Whorf argued that we can't—that language constrains thought—and today their views are known as the Sapir–Whorf hypothesis.

Their ideas are probably best exemplified by the urban myth which claims that because Eskimos have numerous words for snow, they are able to distinguish between many different categories of the fluffy stuff. By contrast, to speakers of other languages, such as English, which have only the one word for snow, snow is, well, just snow.

The evidence is equivocal. An example of how language affects thought comes from studies of the 200-strong Piraha tribe in the Amazon, who have just two numerical words: "hoi" with an accent and "hoi," without, signifying "one" and "two." Any quantities above two they simply refer to as "many." Not surprisingly, the tribe have no currency, but barter goods instead.

The psychologist Peter Gordon of Columbia University in New York City traveled to Brazil and tested the Piraha on a number of numerical matching tasks. For example, he placed a number of batteries in a row and asked the Piraha to lay out the same number. When there were one, two, or three batteries, the tribespeople performed fine, but after that, the greater the number of batteries, the less accurate they became. In other words, the tests appeared to show that the tribe were unable to think about numbers for which they lacked the words.

On the other hand, Stanislas Dehaene and his colleagues at the Collège de France in Paris have found evidence that humans are capable of thinking about concepts for which they lack the words. Dehaene's team studied another Amazonian tribe, the Munduruku, and found that they were able to solve geometric problems and make use of a map even though they have no words for describing spatial relations.

A study providing something of a compromise was published by Susan Hespos and Elizabeth Spelke in 2004. They found that five-month-old babies raised in an English-speaking environment were sensitive to a conceptual distinction that is insignificant in English, but marked in Korean—that is, whether two objects fit together tightly or loosely. Babies generally stop looking at things they are bored of, but Hespos and Spelke found their interest was recaptured if the tightness/looseness between two objects changed. By contrast, adult English speakers didn't notice this difference. The experiment suggests we are able to perceive concepts for which we lack the words, but that the language we learn subsequently shapes which of those concepts remain meaningful to us.

Why Do We Swear?

Why the fu*k do people swear? I'm sorry if that shocked you. But the point was to demonstrate one of the purposes of taboo words, which is to pack a verbally emotional punch. Indeed, neuroimaging studies have shown that the sound of swearwords triggers a response in the emotional part of listeners' brains. It's not entirely clear what gives swearwords their power, but around the world, they usually refer to the same kind of subject matter: sexual relations, genitals, and faeces. However, it takes more than just meaning to make a word taboo—after all, medical terms don't wield the same power. Rather it seems there's some combination of meaning and sounds that makes swearwords special.

The Strange Case of the Language Switchers

It's amazing that people who speak fluently in two languages or more are able to stay focused on one language at a time, without flitting back and forth between the two. One theory for how they do this posits a kind of switch at the front of the brain, which acts as a language controller. Support for the idea comes from reports by Kuan Kho and colleagues of two patients who underwent brain surgery as part of their treatment for epilepsy. One Dutch English bilingual had half his brain anaesthetized, which seemed to flip his switch over to the English position. Attempting to recall a story told to him earlier, he was only able to do so in English. Any Dutch he spoke, he pronounced with an English accent. Then there was the French–Chinese bilingual. His surgeons asked him to count aloud as they prodded his brain with an electrode in an attempt to locate the neural tissue involved in language. He started in French, but then as he reached seven (…cinq, six, sept), the surgeons moved their prodding to the front of his left hemisphere, at which point he involuntarily switched to Chinese (…ba, jiu, shi).

DYSLEXIA

Dyslexia, from the Greek, means literally a difficulty with words. The first description of the condition is often attributed to the English family doctor, W. Pringle Morgan, who reported in 1896 on the case of a 14-year-old boy with "word blindness." Percy was said to be bright and intelligent, yet he struggled to read. Today, dyslexia is thought to affect at least 5 percent of the population. It runs in families, which suggests it has a strong genetic component, and it is often associated with secondary symptoms, such as a difficulty in telling left from right, or postural instability.

A hallmark of the condition is that people with dyslexia struggle with the sounds, known as phonemes, that make up words. If I asked a non-dyslexic to pronounce a nonsense word like "Bagadiboo," they wouldn't have a problem, because they would translate the letters of the word into their appropriate sounds. By contrast, a person with dyslexia would have great difficulty with this.

However, the diagnosis of dyslexia is not quite as straightforward as it might seem. A popular view is that dyslexia is characterized by a level of reading ability that is low relative to the child's overall intelligence. Yet "bad readers" of low general intelligence make the same kind of reading errors, and have the same difficulty with word sounds, as do children with dyslexia. Moreover, dyslexic children and other "bad readers" benefit in the same way from the same kind of interventions, all of which has led some experts to argue that the concept of dyslexia is meaningless. Some children have difficulty learning to read, these experts argue, and they all should be helped as early as possible, regardless of their overall intelligence.

Notwithstanding these issues, the most mainstream and evidence-based treatments for dyslexia place great emphasis on teaching children what are known as phonological skills, to help them learn to process the sounds that words are made of. Other, more controversial treatments tend to focus on the possible causes of the dyslexic child's problems. For example, some experts think that a subset of children with dyslexia have difficulty reading black print on a white background, and so they prescribe colored lenses to help with this. Other experts have linked dyslexia with an abnormality in a part of the brain known as the cerebellum, which is involved with movement control. This theory has led to exercise-based treatments.

Acquired Dyslexia

Although dyslexia is usually considered to be a learning deficit, some people develop dyslexia after suffering brain damage. When this happens, the patient will usually have one of three types of dyslexia. Phonological dyslexia is a problem with translating letters into sounds, of the kind typically seen in children with dyslexia. So-called "surface dyslexia" is the opposite problem. In this case the patient can translate letters into sounds, but they can't read words whole. This means they can pronounce nonsense words like "Bagadiboo," which follow the usual letter-sound correspondence rules, but they can't read irregular words like "pneumonia," which have to be processed whole. Then there's "deep dyslexia," which relates more to a problem with the meaning of words. A patient with this condition might read the word "bus" as "tram" because they will have muddled the two related meanings.

The Boy With Hyperlexia

While children with dyslexia struggle to read, often in spite of having normal intelligence, psychologists in 2006 documented the contrasting case of a four-year-old autistic boy who struggled with most mental tasks except reading. In fact, he was a scarily good reader, even able to pronounce unusual words like "yacht," which don't follow the usual letter-to-sound correspondence rules. According to his mother, the boy started looking through newspapers with zeal before he was even two. Keith Atkin and Marjorie Lorch who documented the case said current accounts of how children learn to read cannot explain this child's literacy abilities. However, they did add that because of his communication difficulties it was unclear how much he understood of what he read.

Jean Piaget and the errors children make

"Assessing the impact of Piaget on developmental psychology is like assessing the impact of Shakespeare on English literature or Aristotle on philosophy—impossible. The impact is too monumental to embrace and at the same time too omnipresent to detect."
Anonymous reviewer of a 1992 journal manuscript on Piaget.

Born in 1896 in Neuchâtel, French Switzerland, Jean Piaget would become one of the most influential thinkers of the twentieth century, and the most highly cited psychologist after Sigmund Freud. He is credited with founding the field of genetic epistemology—the study of how knowledge develops. After a career in which he published 75 books and hundreds of academic papers, his influence on developmental psychology and educational practice is still felt strongly today.

Piaget was a child prodigy who published his first journal paper aged just 11, entitled "On Sighting an Albino Sparrow." He subsequently developed a fascination with mollusks and worked as a teenager as an unpaid assistant in the local natural history museum. In 1918 his study of mollusks led to the award of a doctorate, after which he travelled to Zurich to work with the psychoanalyst Carl Jung. In 1919 he was invited to work in the laboratory of Alfred Binet in Paris, calculating the average intelligence-test performance of children at different ages—it was here that Piaget became fascinated by the mistakes that children make.

In 1923 Piaget married Valentine Chatenay and together they would study their children: Jacqueline, Lucienne, and Laurent. From observing the kind of errors children make, Piaget concluded that they think in a profoundly different way from adults. He believed that children acquire their knowledge about the world by interacting with it, rather like little scientists; and crucially, he thought their understanding of the world advanced in discrete, qualitative stages, such that a child in an earlier stage would be incapable of grasping a concept that required his or her advancement to a later stage.

In 1955 Piaget established the International Center for Genetic Epistemology in Geneva for which he acted as Director until his death in 1980. Piaget was known as "le Patron" by his colleagues and is described as having been hugely charming, but utterly obsessed by his work. He wrote every morning, even when traveling abroad for lectures. Somewhat eccentrically, while lecturing in America, he was said to keep European time, so that everyone there had to arrange their schedules around him.

The Three-Mountain Task

Inspired by the Geneva landscape, Piaget created a three-dimensional model of the large mountain Le Salève across the lake, and two other surrounding peaks. The task for children was to sit in front of the model and try to imagine the view from different perspectives. For example, they might be required to choose the one photo from a selection that matched the view of the mountains from a different angle to their own. Children younger than four don't understand what is being asked of them. Children between four and six understand what's asked of them but are unable to take another person's perspective in this way—thus demonstrating what Piaget called their egocentrism.

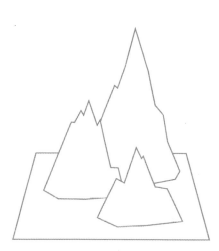

The four stages that Piaget believed all children advance through were known as the sensorimotor stage (birth to about two years), the pre-operational stage (from two to seven years), the concrete operational stage (from seven to twelve years), and the formal operational stage. Piaget believed the stage a child is at can be revealed by the errors they make in his famous tasks, such as the "three-mountain task" and his conservation problems.

Piaget is not without his critics. In some cases, more modern research is showing that the errors children make are not caused by their lack of conceptual understanding, but rather by the limitations of their physical co-ordination. For example, Piaget believed young children are unable to think about objects that they can't see. But the reason infants don't reach for occluded objects may be because they're not capable of reaching around an obstacle, not because they think the object doesn't exist once it is out of sight.

Conservation Problems

Pre-school children are unable to grasp that superficial changes in the appearance of matter don't affect its basic properties. For example, if you pour liquid from a short stubby glass into a tall thin one, a watching pre-school child will likely say there is more liquid in the second glass simply by virtue of the level being higher. They make similar errors with counters—if you spread out counters on a table, the young child will mistakenly think they must have grown in number.

CREATIVITY

Creativity isn't just about composing a groovy tune or painting a sublime landscape—it's also about breaking new ground and considering problems in innovative and useful ways. After all, where would human civilization be today if people had always accepted the status quo?

Creativity tends to work in three stages: there's the preparation stage which involves studying a problem from as many different angles as possible. Next is the incubation period. Novel ideas rarely arrive on demand. In fact they often come once you've stopped thinking about a problem deliberately, and your unconscious mind has had time to work behind the scenes. The third and final stage is the "Aha!" or "Eureka" moment of insight.

It is usually the Eureka moment that we read about in biographies or interviews, which is what gives rise to the popular illusion of effortless creativity. Nobel prize winner Kary Mullis said his idea for the polymerase chain reaction, an innovation that has revolutionized biological research and that underpins genetic fingerprinting, came to him suddenly when driving home one day. Michael Jackson says that many of his classic hits fell into his lap, as if they were a gift from God.

Who Can Be Creative?

A myth that deserves debunking is the idea that some people are capable of being creative while others aren't. Anyone can be creative and creativity can be nurtured. That said, creative types do tend to show certain characteristics.

Intelligence usually plays a part but it is not sufficient for attaining creativity. In fact, extremely high scorers on intelligence tests tend to lack creativity, probably because they have mastered a convergent style of thinking that leads them to zoom in on the right answer, whereas creativity depends on a divergent thinking style— often referred to as lateral thinking, or thinking outside the box.

Creative people tend to be curious and inquisitive. We all have to filter out irrelevant information, otherwise we'd be swamped by data overload, but research shows creative characters have less strict filters. This could help explain the observed association between creativity and psychosis. Some experts have argued that a flexible thinking style combined with an openness to sensory experience can lead to creativity when successfully channelled, but to mental illness if it becomes overwhelming.

MEASURE YOUR CREATIVITY

Go head to head with a friend and see who is the more creative:

1. Take two minutes to write down as many uses as you can for a paper clip.

2. Which one word can form a compound word or two-word phrase with: **(a)** falling, actor, dust?

   Which one word can do the same with: **(b)** room, blood, salts?

This is known as a Remote Associates Test and is used in many psychology experiments on creativity.

3. Take two minutes to write a story involving the words: politician, Jupiter, egg shell.

ANSWERS

(1) the best way to gauge your performance is to see how many uses you came up with compared with your friend(s). If you're feeling really competitive, you might also consider getting a third party to rate the uses for their quality. Also, type "paper clip uses" into a search engine to find plenty of ideas for uses that you missed. (2) (a) star, (b) bath. (3) There obviously isn't a right or wrong answer for this test, but again you could consider getting a third party to rate the quality of the stories you and your friend came up with.

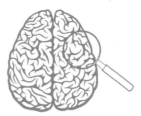

Another myth is that creative people are lazy, tending to lie back and wait for big ideas to hit them. The truth is the opposite. Creative people tend to be extremely well read and informed on the topics that interest them. Creativity is about bringing ideas together in new ways, so the more raw material that is available to a thinker, the more likely they are to come up with a novel and useful idea.

The Neuroscience of Creativity

Mounting evidence suggests that the kind of divergent thinking required for creativity is handled largely by the right hemisphere of the brain. Patients with a rare type of dementia known as fronto-temporal dementia, which particularly affects the left hemisphere, often show enhanced creativity. It's as though their right hemisphere has been released from suppressive supervision by the more logical, literal left hemisphere. Supporting this account are studies by Edward Bowden and colleagues showing that solutions reached via creative insight are associated with increased activity in the right hemisphere. Moreover, people can read more quickly solutions to problems they weren't able to solve, when they are presented in their left visual field (processed by the right hemisphere) as opposed to their right visual field. This suggests the right hemisphere was closer to reaching the answer than the left hemisphere was.

NUMBER SENSE AND NUMBER BLINDNESS

In the same way that some people have a problem with reading, often out of keeping with their overall intelligence, others appear to have a specific deficit when it comes to even the most simple acts of mental arithmetic. People with dyscalculia, as it's known, struggle to answer 5 + 2. Some might even have difficulty if you asked them to say whether the answer is in the ball park of say 40 or 50—they lack that gut feeling of numerical size that most of us take for granted.

Meaning literally to "count badly," from the Greek, dyscalculia is thought to affect around 5 percent of the population, yet is barely heard of relative to its better-known cousin dyslexia. A skill that is often lacking in people with dyscalculia is known as subitizing—the ability to grasp in an instant, without the need for counting, how many items there are in a group of four or less.

Brain-imaging studies carried out in the last few years have revealed that children with dyscalculia have structural and functional abnormalities in a part of

the brain called the intra-parietal sulcus—a region in the parietal lobe, toward the rear of the head, which probably acts as a kind of number-processing module.

This idea was backed up by a transcranial magnetic stimulation (TMS) study in 2007 that involved presenting "normal" participants and dyscalculics with numbers that differed in their physical size (in other words, how BIG they were written), their numerical size, or both. The participants' task was to say in each case which was the bigger of the two numbers, based on

17, 18, 19, 20, 21, 2

physical or numeral size, depending on the trial. As you can imagine, the "normal" participants found the task easier when both the physical size and numerical size of each number were congruent. Crucially, however, when TMS was applied to their intraparietal sulcus, thus temporarily interfering with processing in that region, they no longer benefited from the numerical and physical size of each number being congruent—that is, their performance resembled that of the dyscalculics.

Becoming Rain Man

Remarkably, this same technique of using TMS to temporarily "knock out" a localized area of the brain has also allowed researchers to induce a rare counting ability in normal participants. Do you remember that scene in the film *Rain Man*, in which the autistic character played by Dustin Hoffman immediately recognizes how many cocktail sticks have fallen on the ground? It's almost like an extreme version of the subitizing ability we discussed above. Well, in 2006 psychologist Allan Snyder induced an inferior version of this ability in 10 out of 15 normal participants. The participants watched as dozens of blobs appeared on a computer screen for just one and a half seconds. Their task was to estimate how many blobs, from 50 to 150, had appeared. For example, before the TMS, one woman made 20 guesses and each time she was more than 5 away from the true answer.

Then Snyder applied TMS to the front region of her left temporal lobe, near the ear. Immediately after receiving the TMS, she made 6 out of 20 estimates that were within 5 blobs of the true answer. Not quite *Rain Man*, but the TMS certainly brought the woman closer to his abilities. The researchers said that inhibiting activity in the left temporal lobe shut down the participants' natural tendency to group the blobs into distinct patterns, thus allowing their brain's number module to process the raw sensory data.

Is There Really a Mental Number Line?

Psychologists and philosophers have long held the belief that when we think about numbers we refer to a mental number line, stretching from lower numbers at one end to higher numbers at the other. For years the idea seemed difficult to test, but in 1993 Stanislas Dehaene and colleagues asked people to respond with their right or left hand according to whether a digit was odd or even. A key pattern to emerge was that the participants were quicker to respond to larger numbers with their right hand and to smaller numbers with their left hand. The researchers argued that this was because responding to a larger number is easier with the right hand, as the number is represented mentally toward the right of an imaginary number line, and vice versa for small numbers—an effect they dubbed the "spatial numerical association of response codes effect" or SNARC.

2, 23, 24, 25, 26, 27

Cognition

THE PROBLEM:

Chad Bones, a British spy, has been taken captive. Luckily, he strikes up a rapport with the terrorist ring-leader after they discover a mutual love of Manchester United. The terrorist gives Bones a chance to escape. Four cards with a letter on one side and a picture on the other are placed in the sand. The top faces show: the letter A, the letter M, a skull, a butterfly. "If a card has a vowel on one side," the terrorist snarls, "then that means it has a skull on the other. Which card or cards must you turn over to test whether I speak the truth?"

THE METHOD:

Bones can't believe his luck, this seems like an impossibly easy question. He reaches one of his trembling, bloodied hands toward the card showing the letter A. Surely if he turns the card and it shows anything other than a skull, he will have revealed the terrorist's statement to be a lie. Just as Bones is about to flip the card, the terrorist offers him a clue: "Mr Bones, remember, I want you to turn only the cards that must be revealed to test the truth of my statement."

Bones thinks for a moment. A drop of sweat sluices down his nose and lands with a patter on the "A" card. Bones is convinced this is one of the cards he must turn over. He reaches for the card and flips it to reveal a skull. Grinning, the terrorist grabs the turned card and rips into pieces. "OK, Bones," he says. "Any others?"

Bones eyes the remaining cards and his attention is caught immediately by the card that shows a skull. The scum-bag terrorist specifically said cards with a vowel on one side have a skull on the other. If he turns this skull card and finds a consonant, he reasons that this will expose the statement as a lie. Bones flips the skull card with a flourish, already excited at the prospect of freedom.

THE SOLUTION:

The card shows the letter D. "D for die," barks the terrorist leader, laughing. "Mr Bones, you have failed my challenge." Unbeknown to Bones, the thug sitting in front of him is well-read in psychology and the challenge was a version of the famous Wason Card Selection Task named after the late British psychologist Peter Wason.

The vast majority of people make the same mistake as Bones. By turning over the skull card (or equivalent), he and they are demonstrating what's known as the "confirmation bias." This is our tendency to seek out information that supports a pre-existing belief.

Turning the skull card to reveal a vowel would have provided support for the terrorist's initial statement, but the discovery of a consonant does not in fact refute it. The terrorist said originally that all cards with a vowel on one side have a skull on the other. But this doesn't mean that all cards with a skull on one side have to have a vowel on the other. So it's still consistent with the terrorist's statement for there to be a consonant on one side and a skull on the other.

Bones should have turned over the card with a butterfly. Turning this card to discover a vowel on the other side would have refuted the terrorist's initial statement. Chad Bones was never seen again. If only he'd taken psychology in spy school.

Chapter

4

Affect

All can be going swimmingly in life and yet

for some people a dark cloud of misery lingers.

Meanwhile others seem to enjoy a sunny outlook,

no matter the obstacles life throws in their path.

This chapter is about our emotional lives, and

how our thinking styles and habits affect

the way we feel.

Have you ever had a "good hair day" on a day when you were depressed? It's not likely. More often, the day when you hit a traffic jam is the same day that your boss is intolerable, the kids are obnoxious, the drilling outside your office is louder than usual, and so on… How many times have we said to ourselves, "Why can't something good just happen when I really need it to?" Neuroscience, unfortunately, doesn't wire us to work this way. The term "state of mind" emerges from the realities of how our brain works…

The next time you notice that you are in an especially good mood, sit down and make a list of all the things that have gone right for you lately, all the things you are happy about. The chances are that your positive frame of mind will generate a long list of great things. Then, the next time you are feeling especially negative or cranky, repeat this exercise.

Now, it is more likely that the list will be much more difficult to create a second time. Go ahead and bring out your first list,

and you may find yourself trying to negate and discredit all the happy perceptions your earlier good mood had produced.

The Meaning of Moods

The reason that we can see the good in everything when we are happy, but only the bad side of things when we are upset or angry is that individual emotions feed into the longer-term state of mind commonly called a mood. Also, alongside these psychological factors that influence your mood, are biological ones such as health, diet, and biorhythms.

Our present mood affects which other memories are most readily accessible—known as mood-dependent memory—so that when we are in a good mood, we might recall good memories, and vice versa. Thinking about a lost loved one, for example, evokes sadness and this can trigger other sad memories. Suddenly we're thinking about the ended romance, the lost job, and so on. No wonder we can fall easily into a "woe is me" attitude as one sad thought cascades into many sad thoughts and feelings.

It is also interesting that our moods can alter the accuracy of our recall—an effect that is known as mood-congruent memory. This means that we are more likely to be accurate in our recollections if our current mood matches the emotional content of the memories we summon.

Both of these effects make it is easy to perceive what is really a very subjective interpretation of our overall experience as being the whole truth, and nothing but.

What Can You Do?

Knowing that emotion begets emotion helps combat the idea that our current thoughts are our one and only reality. However, psychologist Robert Thayer also offers some practical advice, finding that the best way to improve your mood involves "a combination of relaxation, stress management, cognitive control, and exercise."

THE DURABILITY BIAS—A THOUGHT EXPERIMENT

So, does the fact that our emotions are not set responses to particular triggers mean we are all at the mercy of our moods? If something bad happens, do we run the risk of spiraling into depression? Predict how long you might anticipate feeling bad if the following events occurred:

(a) Your team lost the championship.
(b) Your significant other left you.
(c) You lost your job.

The good news is that researchers have found that when people predict how long they will feel bad after a negatively perceived event, they overestimate the duration of the emotional impact. Whatever our emotions, although we have ups and downs, we tend to return to a neutral "home" position within a relatively short period of time. This effect is referred to as the Durability Bias, a concept first described by Daniel Gilbert and Timothy Wilson (author of the book *Strangers to Ourselves*, which discusses the phenomena mentioned on page 52).

The inaccuracy of our predictions is linked to our tendency is to be overly focused on the here and now, and the concepts of alternate future possibilities tend not to enter our minds. Wounds do fade, and there will be another season. There can be another love, and maybe your new job will be much better than your old one. People who tend to show greater flexibility and adaptability in their views and who tend to think of alternate possibilities as exciting also report greater levels of enjoyment.

However, in spite of this tendency for people to return to the "middle ground," the greater the disruption to the neutral emotion, and the more often a person stays in the negative processing state, the more difficult it can be for them to return to a balanced state of perception. These are tendencies that can be seen in mood and personality disorders—keeping a person's state of mind in an irrational or unbalanced orientation of perception. This can make them feel as if their reality is "all or nothing," either all good or all bad, and nothing between.

HOW EMOTIONS AFFECT US Part 2

The way emotions affect us is key to our understanding of psychology. However, these theories have changed over the years—even though the ideas of Freud's ego, id, and superego or terms such as "repression" or "Oedipus complex" are still part of a general mainstream body of knowledge. A brief summary of this progression follows:

Q: Why are we all so unhappy? What is the reason behind irrational behavior?

A: Throughout various schools of psychological thought emerge various theories on the cause of "maladaptive behavior." Psychodynamic theory is the classification of approaches to therapy that share an underlying agreement that human behavior is largely motivated by unconscious processes, (processes outside of our immediately accessible sphere of awareness). In these theories, there is an assumption of a set of universal principles that exist and explain personality development and behavior. Development early in the lifespan has a profound effect on the adult one becomes, and gaining insight into the unconscious conflict is a large component of psychotherapy.

For Sigmund Freud, maladaptive behavior was the result of an unconscious unresolved conflict that occurred during childhood. He believed that anxiety is the basis of all neurosis, and maladaptive "defense mechanisms" are faulty ways in which the personality tries to avoid the anxiety experience. For Freud, personality is dictated on the basis of biological drives and the inner conflict is a result of

modulating biological drives. With time, theorists dissented from Freud's ideas that behavior is entirely at the mercy of biological urges, and asserted the influences of society, relationships, and free will (or conscious control) on behavior and personality.

Alongside Sigmund Freud famous psychodynamic theorists include his daughter Anna Freud, Melanie Klein, Margaret Mahler, Harry Stack Sullivan, Erich Fromm, and Carl Jung.

Q: So, I am at the mercy of "healing my inner child" after all?

A: No. Ensuing movements in psychology emerged that focused largely on the "here and now" of experience. Some theorists believe it is not at all necessary to understand the "whys" of how things got to be this way for a person to be able to change the maladaptive behavior, but instead emphasize developing solutions and focusing on motivation.

The Behaviorists

Some approaches to therapy focus completely on achieving specific changes in behavior. Classic and operant conditioning are well-known examples of behavioral modification theory. Within classical conditioning, Nobel prize winner Ivan Pavlov's experiments with dogs showed that after a bell was consistently paired with food, dogs would salivate upon hearing the bell even when no food was present.

Operant conditioning, most associated with B.F. Skinner, associates behavioral conditioning with stimuli that are learned instead of innate reactions (as is a salivation response to food). For example, if a woman receives treatment at a hospital which is an anxiety-provoking experience, subsequent anxiety may be aroused when visiting the hospital, even for an innocuous event such as visiting a friend there who has just delivered a baby.

Treatment through behavioral modification is widely applied in the treatment of phobias and anxiety disorders, can be useful for stopping smoking, and is quite regularly utilized in resolving behavioral difficulties with children. The use, for example, of a "token economy" where a child receives a star or other reward to enforce proper behavior (or removing a reward at undesirable behavior, such as "grounding") is an example of behavioral modification through operant conditioning, pairing environmental stimuli to reinforce desired behavioral results.

Systematic desensitization is an approach based on classical conditioning theory most commonly used to treat anxiety disorders. Here, a hierarchical approach of applying gradually more intensive and repeated exposure to an anxiety-provoking stimulus is paired with relaxation training, deconstructing the evoking process, by means of gradual exposure (using real or guided imagery) in a safe environment. The stimulus is paired with the experience of nondisastrous results when exposure to the imagined danger does not occur, gradually extinguishing the anxiety response.

Cognitive Behavior

The most common approach to psychotherapeutic treatment is that of cognitive behavioral therapy (CBT). Cognitive behavioral therapy emerged out of growing dissatisfaction with what seemed to be shortsightedness of parts of both the behavioral and the psychodynamic models. CBT combines the roles that cognitive factors play in shaping behavior in these theories. These approaches examine patterns of mistaken belief and irrational thought, and their effect on a person's misguided emotional state, and resulting behavior.

Albert Ellis, who created "rational emotive therapy," and Aaron Beck, who founded cognitive behavioral therapy and developed the "Beck depression inventory," a tool for measuring severity of depression, are two well-known therapists from the CBT movement.

EMOTION IN THE BRAIN

Emotions are the most guiding and pervasive force behind individual psychology. They influence our decisions, our ideas of right and wrong, our relationships, the health of our bodies, and they influence our perceptions from the most subtle areas of our lives to the most all-consuming. Indeed, it would be nearly impossible to find a sphere of cognition immune to the influence of emotions.

UNDERSTANDING THE THOUGHT–EXPERIENCE CONNECTION

True or False?

1. A lovers' quarrel can delay the healing of a wound.
2. When a patient believes that something he or she is given will relieve pain, the body actually releases the pain-killing endorphins even when a placebo is administered.
3. One bad thing happening neurologically codes how our brain will rank other unrelated events and perceptions.
4. Under clinical hypnosis, someone who is told he or she is being touched by a burning-hot object can produce a blood blister when actually touched by an object at room temperature.

SCORING

Amazingly these are all true. The connection between thoughts and experiences is so strong it has physical effects.

But what are emotions? Where do they come from? Can we control them, or do they control us? Are emotions a matter of perception? Do we have the power to change our emotions, and thereby change our thoughts and our experience? Or must we begin by changing our thoughts, and thereby change our emotional state?

Making Emotions Real

Can you think of a time when a coach told you to visualize yourself hitting the home run before a big game, when a friend "talked you out of a bad mood," or when you aced a test because you "knew" you could do it? The scientific reality is that our body responds to mental input as if it were physically real—images create bodily responses just as if the experiential stimuli have occurred. Electrocardiogram measurements in a number of studies, including those by Erfani and Efanian, show that mental rehearsal sends the same messages to your brain as when you are actually doing the real exercise.

The implications of these realities are astounding. Scientists have a good understanding of the neurological systems behind emotion and feelings. Dopamine is associated with experiencing pleasure, happiness, and reward, low serotonin is implicated in depression, and endorphins are produced and released in the brain after exercise, sex, eating chocolate, viewing beautiful art, watching a touching dramatic scene, or even listening to an evocative piece of music. The fact that training our thinking mechanisms can guide physiological processes allows ourselves greater responsibility for actions relating to our own success and well-being.

Positive Psychology

Positive psychology (the branch of psychology dedicated to optimal experience) encourages people to focus their daily lives on getting the most rewarding experiences, by learning to manage the daily rhythms of life. By being able to concentrate on these rhythms, a person can achieve a sense of "flow"—a concept described by Croatian psychologist Mihály Csíkszentmihályi—in which goals are challenging but achievable, and a person's actions are focused but apparently effortless. It is a concept that is perhaps most often described in relation to sports stars, who, after a particularly good performance, claim to have been "in the zone."

EXAMINING THE GOOD, HAVING A BAD DAY

When someone asks me "How are you?" I tend to answer:

(a) "I'm fine"—no matter how I am feeling, it's just a greeting, not a real question.

(b) "Not that well…" followed by venting all the current things I am struggling with.

(c) "Great"—no matter what complaints I may have, my life is full of blessings that I appreciate.

How many times a day does one ask and get asked that question, "How are you?" And how do we determine the answer? Our state of being at any given time is one of the most crucial factors of our experience and our awareness. But is our experience of ourselves and our situation objective or subjective? Could one person's "good" be the exact equivalent of another person's "bad?" Can one person be destined to a chemistry of woe and disappointment while another is blessed with fulfillment and joy?

Try to think of a time where your affect (feelings) didn't match up with your perception of an event. Perhaps you received some excellent news, but felt unable to truly experience the joy. Or perhaps you may have wondered why something you would have expected to bother you simply rolled off your back. The reality tends to be that we have control of our perceptions, using your answer to the question above as a guide, see if you can identify the shade of the filter through which you tend to view things? It may be that you are able to improve your lot simply by being willing to change your perspective.

FACIAL RECOGNITION

Sono felice di vederli. Je suis heureux de vous voir. Eu sou feliz vê-lo.
I am happy to see you. Italy, France, Portugal, and Britain exist in
relatively close geographical proximity to one another, but if we relied
solely on language to communicate the above message, it is obvious
how difficult things would be. Besides, what does eyesight have to
do with joy?

Fortunately, we determine much of what another person is feeling from the expression on their face. The feelings most often expressed in both literate and preliterate societies are universal in their facial language of communication: anger, disgust, fear, and happiness. But advanced communication and interpretation of emotions requires more than simply the processing of a person's facial expression, and calls for us to accommodate other factors, creating a bigger picture. How do we know not to offer condolences to the person crying next to us at a wedding?

(Unless of course the tears relate to not liking the spouse-to-be or wishing it was them at the altar instead.) We smile when we are happy, but also when we're embarrassed or even resigned. Vocal speed and tone, background, and other personality data are all interwoven in recognition. How does the brain recognize and translate these levels of information to communicate emotionality?

Early visual processing codes spatial relations and configurations of the input. Research has shown that visual sensory input (in this case, the facial expression) is

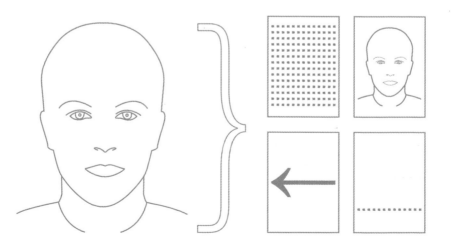

initially processed by coding spatial relation and configuration. It is impossible to determine "angry" eyebrows or an "angry" mouth in isolation from the rest of the face. For example, angry eyebrows, may appear the same as perplexed eyebrows, so a different mouth position may differentiate the two. At the next level of processing, additional stimulus recognition occurs, and things can be classified or placed as belonging to a familiar perceptual category. Semantic processing then occurs, where meaning can be drawn from associations with past experiences, emotions evoked in one's self, context, and background. Finally, naming processes are activated and retrieved ("smile").

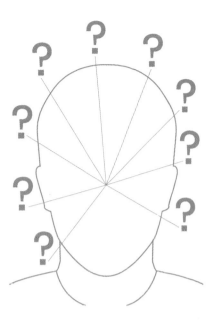

Empathy

The fact that an emotion in another tends to evoke a similar emotion in oneself further helps us categorize the stimuli and "understand" the emotions of one another. In experiential terms, the ramifications of this are complicated. This helps us to understand further why a bad mood can be contagious, and why spending time with less than emotionally healthy people can be dangerous for one's own mental health.

Studies show that the truth behind the old saying "Misery loves company" is more accurately "Misery loves miserable company." When given the choice to be alone or with others, depressed people chose first to be in the company of other similarly struggling people, or secondly to be alone. They did not choose to be around people who were not likewise depressed.

It has been found that people respond more quickly toward those stimuli that evoke positive emotions than stimuli that evoke negative emotions. If that isn't firm

evidence that the best way to get through to someone is not through intimidation or expressing anger, then what is?

Our ability to understand others may literally lie in our ability to understand ourselves, and also in our shared experiences. Interesting examples of this can be found in studies of subjects who had suffered brain damage that left them unable to experience specific emotions. For example, in a study undertaken by British neuropsychologist Andy Calder and colleagues, subjects suffering from Huntington's Disease who were unable to experience disgust also had trouble recognizing facial expressions of disgust.

DEPRESSING COGNITIVE DISTORTIONS Part 1

AN INVENTORY FOR YOUR LIFE

	Strongly Disagree	Disagree	Neutral Feelings	Agree	Strongly Agree
I have a likeable personality.					
I have much to offer to a significant other.					
I have intimate, strong, and equal relationships.					
I am able to communicate and get my needs met.					
I can accept failure in myself and others.					
My friends can depend on me.					
I can depend on my friends.					
I am satisfied with my life.					
I am satisfied with myself.					
I am satisfied with how others treat me.					
I am able to handle difficulties.					
I have found opportunities that suit me.					
I am able to make the best out of a situation.					
When mistakes happen, I am more concerned with figuring out how to fix it than needing to know whose fault it is.					

As we have established, there are patterns in thinking and perception that influence one's overall levels of happiness. the exercise to the left is meant to serve as a guide to explore some of your own tendencies. Review your answers. Are they clustered in any one area? What can this tell you about yourself?

Such inventories are sometimes used by psychotherapists in order to reveal potential depressing cognitive distortions that certain personality types may get trapped in. Here are a few of the more common ones:

Learned Helplessness

One of the most depressing cognitive distortions is that of "learned helplessness," a concept introduced in the late 1960s by Martin Seligman. In a state of learned helplessness a person believes themselves to be stuck in a situation over which they have no control, and that any efforts to improve that situation are futile—so no such attempts are made. However, this sense of helplessness is rarely accurate. Those people with such a perception tend to take little responsibility for their own decisions, may not feel respected, and may hesitate to demand that respect. It may also be difficult for them to express or communicate their inner experiences, and they may feel isolated and that "The world is against them." However, by understanding the nature of the distortion from which they suffer, a person may feel empowered to make some changes, and happiness can often be just a few steps away.

Perfectionism

The pursuit of perfection, for some of us, can render us incapable of enjoying our lives. While a person with a well-balanced personality can accept that he or she may be better at certain things than others, and may derive satisfaction from doing something well, a neurotic perfectionist—as described by Don Hamachek—may in their own mind "never seem to do things good enough to warrant that feeling [of satisfaction]."

The risks associated with perfectionism are many, and it can be an indicator of a number of other problems such as Obsessive Compulsive Disorder (see pages 120–21).

Perfectionism is a dangerous distortion: nothing is ever enough, and nothing is ever good enough. Being patient with ourselves and our lives, and letting where we are and what we have simply be enough, is one of the most important skills to master in the art of achieving happiness.

DEPRESSING COGNITIVE DISTORTIONS Part 2

I Hate You

Another of the most prominent depressing cognitive distortions is the idea that we are at the mercy of others' dislikable traits. While we cannot control other people, we can work on what their behavior brings out in ourselves. That isn't to say that other people are perfect, or that there are no genuinely dislikeable people in the world. However, it might also be worth looking inward. Perhaps you are angry that someone is overly controlling? Are they really—or are you perhaps too easily controlled? The reality is that often when we are drawn into such a state of negative emotion by something in someone else, it frequently relates to something we don't like in ourselves.

While concern about others' well-being is important, depressed people tend to spend an inordinate amount of time worrying about the issues of others, instead of taking care of and focusing on themselves.

Mood-Congruent Behavior

Another powerful cognitive distortion relates to the thought-grouping effect that was discussed earlier (see page 72). Sure enough, studies—including those by Erich Eich and Peter Suedfeld at the University of British Columbia—have shown that

THE LINE DOWN THE MIDDLE OF THE PAPER

Take a blank piece of paper, and draw a vertical line down the middle of the page.

Now, think about your closest relationships: friends, family, colleagues, and so on. On one side of the line, write down all the character traits of each of them that you don't care for. Try to keep it in simple one-word definitions. Go ahead, no-one will know…

Now, on the other side of the page, write out the corresponding, opposite traits. For example, if you wrote "know it all," on one side side write "ignorant" on the other.

When you have your list, separate it into the two halves on either side of the line. Now take a good long look at what you don't like about everyone else. And throw it in the trash.

Now you have the list of negative attributes, see if you recognize these in yourself. It might well be that what you dislike in some other people is actually mirrored by corresponding characteristics in yourself. If this is the case then your sense of helplessness at being the victim of others' personalities could be resolved by the realization that you have the power to make changes within yourself.

people who are in good moods think that they are healthier than they actually are, are overly optimistic about the state of the environment and the economy, and are able to view a poor city riddled with social problems as a "struggling" city as opposed to seeing it as an example of the general state of things, as is the tendency of depressed people. This effect is labeled as mood-congruent behavior.

The upshot of this behavior can be that when we are depressed, we tend to find reasons in our environment to support the depressive cognition, whether they are really there or not.

know it all
demanding

ignorant
passive

WHY DO WE LOVE WHO WE LOVE?

Love has to be blind. In the first stage of falling in love, we idealize our partner. In our mind's eye, we amplify the traits that we are drawn to and focus on that we want to see. We choose to ignore, dismiss, or underemphasize the traits we don't like. This is furthered by the tendency for each of us to "be at our best" at the beginning of the relationship, something for which we then often credit our beloved— how ironic! The majority of new couples also think their relationship is "special" when compared to others, and that they have found something deeper and more intimate than what other couples share. This blind love may serve to allow us to progress to the stages where the following chemistry begins.

WHO DO YOU LOVE

Research has shown who we fall for.

Love yourself? We tend to fall for someone who looks like we do.

Love your daddy? We tend to fall for someone who looks like our parents.

Dr. Martha McClintock at the University of Chicago has carried out studies that show we are also attracted to people who have complementary immune systems to ours, something we subconsciously determine through each other's odor.

At the University of California Albert Mehrabian has also suggested that we assign likeability to others in surprising ways. According to his studies, words play a relatively minor part, and instead some 55 percent of whether we find someone appealing can be attributed to body language, 38 percent to the tone and speed of their voice, and only 7 percent relates to what is actually said.

Love and Chemistry

Predictable patterns of neurochemistry emerge when we are "falling in love," and explain many of the cherished symptoms we equate with this state of being. Not surprisingly, the initial draw to become close to someone is driven by the sex hormones estrogen and testosterone in both men and women.

Love Is a Drug

In the next stage of love, our stress response is activated, which increases our blood pressure and causes our heart to race. We experience higher levels of dopamine, the neurochemical that is responsible for creating the experience of an intense rush of pleasure. This is related to our increased energy, decreased need for sleep or food, focused attention on the other person and the relationship, and the immense satisfaction we take in the small details.

Obsessed With You

When in newfound love, we can't stop ourselves from thinking about the other person. Italian psychologist Donatella Marazziti and her team found that the experience in your mind is related to a decrease in our serotonin levels—to the same level that is seen in people with Obsessive Compulsive Disorder.

Another factor associated with low serotonin is the drive to have more sex, which explains why couples are much more sexually active in the early stages of a relationship—and why, as the relationship continues and serotonin levels normalize, a couple's sex life slows down.

Another key player in the chemistry of love is oxytoxin, one of two hormones thought to be involved in the experience of "attachment." Oxytoxin is a strong hormone released by men and women during orgasm. This explains the tendency towards feeling closer to someone after having sex than would be explained purely through the physical act, intimate as it is. Oxytoxin is likewise released during breastfeeding, contributing to the development of attachment in this process for a mother toward her baby. Researchers found that blocking oxytoxin release in animals causes them to neglect their young, while injecting it in others causes them to protect and nurture the young of another animals.

The second hormone associated with social attachment is revealed in animal studies on the prairie vole. After mating, male and female prairie voles remain together for life, and they are known to have sex much more often than is required simply for reproductive purposes. However, when the hormone vasopressin was blocked in the prairie voles, they quickly lost their devotion to their partner.

Want to Fall in Love?

Well, New York-based psychologist Arthur Arun has found the formula. He had subjects who had never met nor seen one another before reveal very intimate details about their lives for half an hour, then stare silently into one another's eyes for four minutes. A strong majority of the subjects reported feeling deeply attracted to one another after the experiment—amazingly, one couple even went on to get married.

Why not find out for yourself? You may well find that inquiries among your friends, family, and colleagues reveal confessions of intimacies exchanged early in their relationships.

LOVE GONE WRONG

DON'T PET THE BABY

The school of behaviorism was a strong force in psychology between the 1920s and 1970s. Behaviorists concerned themselves only with what could be seen and therefore studied. Thoughts and emotions were not of concern. According to this mindset, ideas like love and affection were not touted as important factors in healthy psychological development. Cuddling and coddling were discouraged, discipline was paramount.

A statement by the president of the American Psychological Association, J.B. Watson, exemplifies the mindset. As a behaviorist who "didn't believe in cognition," he once stated: "When you are tempted to pet your child, remember that mother love is a dangerous instrument."

Psychologist Harry Harlow's classic experiments served as a strong influence in challenging the notions of the behaviorists. His studies involved baby monkeys who were removed from their real mothers and given the option of two "mother" surrogates: one was a cuddly soft cloth mother who had a heat source and a replicated heartbeat, the other a wire mother who provided food. The babies clung to the soft cuddly surrogate mother, ran to her when exposed to fearful stimuli, and drew strength from her presence when threatened by strange objects. They spent little time with the wire, feeding mother.

In a disturbing twist, a more recent study isolated monkeys for the first six months (equivalent to two years in a human lifespan) or raised them with monkeys of their own age, and gave them free access to two sweetened solutions, one of which contained alcohol while the other did not. Motherless monkeys, raised without any adult primates, consumed considerably more alcohol, often to the point of intoxication, than those raised by a mother.

The Maternal Instinct

There has been debate over whether the inclination to care for offspring is hard-wired in the biology of species, or whether it is learned behavior. Harlow also studied monkeys who had been denied maternal care of their own in their relations with their own offspring. He found the motherless mothers were inattentive to their own young, challenging the idea that a mother's instinct is biological, and supporting the idea that it is learned behavior.

Break-Up Blues

Have you ever known someone who couldn't get over a break-up? No matter the amount of time that had passed, your friend simply did not "move on." He or she may have claimed that no-one else lived up to their ex-beloved, or could not find the strength to continue without the other person's presence. In many personalities, the inability to return to one's own sphere of self, after a normal amount of grieving, marks an imbalance in the self.

Break-ups generally involve a degree of rejection, and a study by a team of psychologists at Columbia University revealed that women who "anxiously expect, readily perceive, and overreact to rejection" became more depressed when their partner split up with them, but not when a break-up was mutual or of their own initiation—when compared to those women whose initial fear of rejection was not so great.

So, before you are too quick to accept that it's all about how much your friend misses the other person, ponder the idea that possibly, they just couldn't accept the thought that someone actually left them.

HEALTHY DEPENDENCE, OR CODEPENDENCE

Love can take many forms, and personalities are drawn to each other for a great many reasons, not all of which are healthy. The relationships with the least amount of conflict exist in a balanced state of complementary strengths, and of equal respect. The difference between a healthy dependence and codependence can be difficult to understand.

Which of the following more accurately describes your current or past relationships?

(a) My partner and I have different strengths, but equal respect. We disagree on how things may best be accomplished, but work together to achieve results or compromises.

(b) My partner and I struggle to take care of ourselves without each other, we often face conflict, and it feels like there is a fight for power.

Overly independent personalities may find it difficult to accept or ask for help or let other people be involved, even when it is needed. Overly dependent personalities find it difficult to make their own decisions, have strong opinions, or lead endeavors. Overly controlling personalities may find it difficult to let anyone else have a say or to conceive of things outside of their own sphere of conception. One can easily see how different personality types could fit together, in ways that do not challenge dysfunctional traits, and "enable" each other to continue in maladaptive ways. The bottom line of a healthy romantic relationship is that it exists as a partnership between equals. A queen may date a pauper, but if she chooses to date him, he must be treated with respect and equality.

EMOTIONAL INTELLIGENCE

Emotional intelligence relates not just to your ability to assess and manage your own emotions, but also the ability to relate to the emotions of other individuals and groups. To be "emotionally intelligent" involves thinking more intelligently about emotion, and more emotionally about intelligence.

MOTIVATION
Learned, goal-driven behavior
Biological urges

AFFECT
Emotions
Moods
Feeling states (energy)

COGNITION
Memory
Reasoning
Judgement
Abstract thought

Drives and urges provide the basic motivations for our actions.

Our emotional state (affect) provokes our cognition to meet the requirements of our motivations. Emotional intelligence measures how well the affective sphere functions.

Both conscious and unconscious cognition are used to direct actions in order to fulfill motivations. Measures of intelligence are used to indicate how well the cognitive sphere functions.

Emotion: Guide or Interference?

Put your self in the following situation: You are a director of a not-for-profit legal agency; your job involves advocacy for adolescent victims of family conflict. You hold a high-profile job, and involves working with government leaders, attorneys, legislators, children, and families. You have run a successful program, and one of your biggest accomplishments has been an anger-management education campaign, which has led to a high percentage of children being able to be reunited with their families. While it is your job to attend to the needs of all parties involved equally, a six-year-old girl named Charlie has taken to sneaking into your office when she is in the agency, and leaving you notes with stickers thanking you for returning her to her parents. At one of the biggest networking events of the year, you hear a loud crash followed by a commotion. You are the closest person, so you rush over to see what happened. You see little Charlie with plates full of ice cream all around her, you are about to burst into laughter at the sweet little girl, covered in sweets, when her father grabs her aggressively by her arm and starts screaming at her about her clumsiness. You run to Charlie's side, grab her in your arms, and start screaming at her father, "Didn't you learn anything? How dare you talk to her this way!" The state senator happens to walk by just now, witnessing you red-faced and hot-tempered, screaming at a grown man.

Is This Reaction Emotionally Intelligent?

Your behavior is certainly understandable, protecting a little girl against what seems a direct threat. But was it encompassing a higher degree of thinking: showing the ability to incorporate the needs of all parties involved in the situation? Did you combine your cognitive abilities with your emotional guidance?

It is difficult to determine one emotionally intelligent way of dealing with such a situation. Certainly rationality points toward the protection of the little girl, but it also requires the preservation of other people's confidence in your ability to manage conflict.

Often our emotions seem to "get the better of us" and take a direct path to the action part of our brain. Sometimes emotions seem to bypass the cognitive sphere entirely, leaving us to wonder retrospectively, "Why on earth did I do that?"

So what, then, is the purpose of emotions? Are they meant to be an innate direction signal for behavior, and if so, why do things seem to go awry? Think about a time when you yourself simply "got carried away," whether by love, anger, pity, or any other emotion.

Emotional Intelligence, Mood, and Self-Esteem

Two noteworthy studies investigated the relationship between emotional intelligence and mood, and between emotional intelligence and self-esteem. The results indicated that higher emotional intelligence was associated with a characteristically positive mood, higher self-esteem, and better emotional regulation after exposure to conflict.

This is interesting when you realize that other forms of intelligence do not strictly correlate like this; for example, individuals with Down's Syndrome, who score low on intelligence testing, often have very positive mood states and good self-esteem.

We rely on our skills of emotional intelligence. Sometimes we act more intelligently than at other times, and some of us seem to possess a greater degree of emotional intelligence than others. However, there is hope for us all: just like any form of intelligence, emotional intelligence can be learned.

LAZARUS THEORY

There are a number of different theories that postulate different sequences of cause and effect between motivation, cognition, affect, and physical effect. For example, the theory put forward by Richard Lazarus states that a thought must come before any emotion or physiological arousal. In other words, you must first think about your situation before you can experience an emotion.

Affect

THE PROBLEM:

You have a first date this evening at a fashionable restaurant in town. That's the good news. The bad news is you're feeling painfully nervous, and thanks to work stress and a leak at home, you're mightily fed up too. Thing is, you don't want your date to get the impression that you're an anxious grump. What psychological insights can you use to control your emotions and ensure you make a good impression?

THE METHOD:

We usually think of emotional feelings coming first and then the behavioral and bodily effects appear as a consequence. You cry because you're feeling sad. You're scared so you run. Today you fear appearing nervous and moody because that's how you feel. But what if the causal direction can flow the other way? This idea was proposed by the Godfather of American psychology William James at the end of the nineteenth century. He gave the example of a person running from a bear in a wood. The person runs from the bear, James said, and it is the act of running that provokes the feeling of being scared. This became known as the James-Lange theory of emotion, incorporating the name of Carl Lange, another nineteenth-century thinker who proposed similar ideas.

Although we now know that other multiple factors are at play in the experience of emotion, recent years have seen a proliferation of evidence in partial support of the James-Lange theory. For instance, there's research showing that the simple act of smiling can lead some people to feel happier. People pulling a smiling face also tend to recall more positive events from memory when asked to reminisce, as compared with people holding a neutral expression. There's even evidence that people who've had botox experience less intense emotions, presumably because they're unable to pull emotional facial expressions. Another line of research has shown that adopting a star-shaped power posture allows people to endure more pain because it helps them feel more in control. These effects are thought to work because performing certain behaviours and facial expressions leads to bodily feedback that reaches the brain, actually affecting how we feel.

THE SOLUTION:

You can exploit these psychological processes to help you prepare for your date and increase the chance you'll enjoy the experience once it's underway. Richard Wiseman, the professor for the public understanding of psychology at the University of Hertfordshire in the UK,

calls this the "as-if" principle. Behave as if you are happy and confident—smile and hum merrily to yourself as you get ready for the evening—and you will likely find that you start to feel happy too. How we interpret bodily sensations is another important element of emotion. Try to think of those butterflies in your stomach as a source of excitement rather than fear.

Once you're at the restaurant with your date, you can carry on practising the as-if principle. Unfold your arms and adopt a relaxed posture. Focus on the present and leave your worries behind—there's nothing more you can do about them right now anyway. Behave as if you're at ease and you'll start to feel less up-tight. Another tactic is to focus your attention on the other person. Remind yourself that they are probably nervous too. Make some effort to try to help them feel more comfortable and you'll likely find that you become less aware of your own anxiety. Plus, if you help them relax a little, they'll be grateful and the atmosphere will lighten further. Go on, smile—you really are going to have a great time!

5

The Social Self

We're a profoundly social species and some of
the most famous experiments in psychology have
been concerned with the way we relate to each
other. Why do we follow orders? Why is there so
much prejudice in the world when we are all
members of the same human race? We'll look at
these questions as well as providing tips for
improving our more personal relationships.

PREJUDICE

How would you sum up social history in nine words? How about: People form into groups and compete with other groups? Okay, that doesn't cover everything, but there's no question that, from families to nation-states, the tendency of people to form themselves into social groups has had a profound impact on our history. Group membership brings obvious benefits in terms of co-operation and teamwork, but an unfortunate side effect is that instead of seeing each other as individuals, we make judgments and assumptions about others based on their group membership.

Are You In My Gang or Aren't You?

Henri Tajfel and colleagues demonstrated the power of group identity in a classic study published in 1971. School children were allocated to one of two groups based purely on their preference for one of two abstract artists: Paul Klee and Vassilij Kandinsky. When each child subsequently chose how to distribute money between a pair of their anonymous peers, identified only by their membership of the Klee or Kandinsky group, they showed a consistent tendency to go for the option that meant the child in their group received more money.

This instinct for group loyalty is thought to lie at the heart of much of the prejudice found in today's world. Historically, it may have been helpful for our ancestors to be able to identify fellow group members according to certain markers such as clothing or symbols (skin color would probably have varied little or not at all between neighboring tribes). The trouble is, we continue to use such short-cuts today even when they are most often meaningless. Biology shows, for example, that there is more genetic variation between members of the same racial group than there is between members of different racial groups. Unfortunately, the social cues that we use tend to be those that are most crude, such as age, gender, and race.

You're Disgusting

What's more, new research is showing that our obsession with who is or isn't in our group may be driven in part by the emotion of disgust. In the same way that visceral disgust leads us to avoid ingesting old or contaminated food, the same emotion may underlie our desire to keep social outsiders, with their alien mores and beliefs, separate from our own group. Supporting this comes research showing that people who are more conservative, for example, espousing anti-immigration policies, also tend to be more disgust-prone, based on their agreement with statements like: "I never let

MEASURE YOUR SOCIAL ATTITUDES

A difficulty psychologists have when researching prejudice is that people will often censor their attitudes so as to make them seem socially acceptable. One method believed to overcome this problem is called the Implicit Association Test, many examples of which are freely accessible on-line.

The idea is that the ease with which we associate two categories can affect how quickly we respond when we have to use the same computer key to respond to the sight of those two categories. So, for example, if we hold strong conservative views, we might be expected to respond more slowly when using the same key for positive words (for example, "good") and supposedly liberal behaviors (for example, homosexuality), than if the experimental set-up meant we were able to use the same key for negative words and liberal values or behaviors.

A criticism of the technique is that rather than reflecting our own attitudes, the speed of our response can be influenced by how often we encounter the pairing of certain categories and value judgments in everyday life. For example, we might often read about how bad it is that more teenagers are falling pregnant, thus influencing our response times, even though we might not hold that judgment ourselves.

any part of my body touch the toilet seat in public restrooms."

Brain-imaging research is even showing that we are prone to viewing members of some social groups as less than human—a finding that could help explain humankind's capacity for such cruelty to others. Lasana Harris and Susan Fiske scanned the brains of university students as they looked at pictures of people from different social groups. The sight of sporting heroes, the elderly, and businessmen all triggered activity in the medial prefrontal cortex—an area of the brain associated with thinking about other people or oneself. By contrast, the sight of homeless people or drug addicts failed to provoke activity in this area, and in fact triggered a response in the areas of the brain related to disgust.

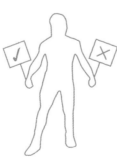

OBEDIENCE TO AUTHORITY

Obedience is vital to the existence of a civilized society. If the majority of people chose to disobey the rule of law, then we'd be living in anarchy. But obedience has a dark side. To some extent, it was the willingness of ordinary people to obey orders that resulted in some of history's worst atrocities.

A Shocking Experiment

One of the most famous psychology experiments of all time investigated how far people will go in their obedience to authority. In 1961 Stanley Milgram invited male participants to a Yale University lab to take part in what they were told was a study of the effects of punishment on learning. Their task was to apply electric shocks of increasing voltage to another participant (who was really an actor) whenever he got an answer in a verbal memory test wrong. The participants were reassured that though the shocks could be extremely painful, they would cause no permanent harm.

Shocks were applied by flicking a line of 30 switches, which increased in 15-volt increments up to 450 volts. The switches were also labelled in groups of four, from "Slight Shock" all the way up to "Danger: Severe Shock," with the final two groups beyond 330 volts simply marked "XXX."

The participants watched as the man playing the role of learner was strapped to a chair. The participants then returned to the adjacent room where the shock controls were housed. From the outset, the learner answered many questions incorrectly, so the participants were instructed to keep cranking up the shocks.

At 300 volts, the learner pounded the wall in protest. At 315 volts, he pounded again before ceasing to give any further answers. Beyond this point he fell completely silent.

The experimenter, a stern man in a gray lab coat, told the researchers to treat a non-response as a wrong answer and to keep increasing the voltage. There were 40 participants from a range of professions, aged between 20 and 50. How many of them do you think continued applying electric shocks right up to the highest level? Would you have continued until the end?

The answer is that 26 out of the 40 participants delivered the highest shock— two categories higher than "Danger: Severe Shock"! Milgram reported similar results in further experiments; however, it has been difficult for others to replicate his work because of ethical issues. The participants found the experiment extraordinarily stressful. Many were trembling and sweating; others had nervous laughing fits. One man had such violent convulsions that the experiment had to be aborted.

The impact of the experiment on both academic psychology and popular culture has been immense. Milgram conducted his experiments just months after the trial of Nazi war criminal Adolf Eichmann. More

HOW OBEDIENT TO AUTHORITY ARE YOU?

1. I was suspended from school for bad behavior. YES/NO
2. I feel slightly nervous when I see police officers. YES/NO
3. I think rules exist to be broken. YES/NO
4. I would never talk loudly in a library. YES/NO
5. I often take short-cuts across the grass. YES/NO
6. I think it is important for the country to have a strong leader. YES/NO
7. No-one ever bosses me around. YES/NO
8. I would never park in a prohibited space. YES/NO

recently, the U.S. troops responsible for the prisoner abuse at the Abu Ghraib camp in Iraq claimed they were following orders, so the experiment and the questions it raises about obedience remain as topical as ever.

Experiments in Virtual Reality

In 2006, psychologists at University College London recreated Milgram's classic experiment in virtual reality. Participants applied shocks to a computer-animated woman whenever she made errors in a memory test. Rather than being a test of obedience, the objective of the experiment was really to see just how immersive and realistic virtual reality can be.

Remarkably, several of the participants opted to stop the experiment before delivering the strongest shock, and measures of their heart rate and sweating showed they were clearly stressed by the experience.

ISSUES WITH GROUP BRAINSTORMING

Imagine you and your friends were asked to come up with as many ways as possible to increase tourism to your home town. How would you organize yourselves? You might think your best bet would be to sit down together and have a good old brainstorming session. But in fact the research consistently shows that doing so would hamper your creativity. You'd be much better off if you each went away to think on your own, only reuniting to pool your suggestions.

In 1987 Michael Diehl and Wolfgang Stroebe listed 22 prior studies that compared the productivity of brainstorming groups with the productivity of groups in which team members worked alone before pooling their ideas. The message was clear: 18 out of 22 of the studies showed that the groups where members worked alone came up with more ideas than the brainstorming groups.

Why Is Brainstorming Still So Popular?

According to the Dutch psychologist Bernard Nijstad, when we participate in a group brainstorming session, we spend a lot of time waiting for other people to speak, which takes the pressure off us, and we also come away with a sense that plenty of ideas have been bounced around. By contrast, when we work alone, we place a constant pressure on ourselves to come up with ideas. And if we're creatively sterile for more than a few moments, it can leave us with a sense that we are failing. It is this difference in what it feels like to work alone compared with in a brainstorming group that Nijstad thinks underlies people's continuing faith in brainstorming.

A study Nijstad completed with colleagues in 2006 seems to support this. They asked dozens of university students to work either alone or in groups to come up with ways to boost tourism to Utrecht. Afterward, those students who completed the task in groups were far more satisfied with the ideas they'd come up with and felt like they'd suffered fewer failures of creativity than did the students who'd completed the task alone.

Other ways in which brainstorming can feel more effective than working alone include memory confusion—that is, retrospectively mistaking other people's ideas for your own; and the process of "social comparison"—when we see how difficult other people are finding it to come up with ideas it can make us feel better about our own performance.

Three Is the Magic Number

When it comes to logic-based problem-solving as opposed to idea generation, three-person groups work best. In a 2006 paper, Patrick Laughlin and colleagues tested the performance of two-, three-, four-, and five-person groups on letter–number logic problems, in which participants had to work out which letters corresponded to which numbers using as few questions as possible. The three-, four-, and five-person groups consistently out-performed the same numbers of people working alone. Crucially, however, the four- and five-person groups were no better than the three-person groups, suggesting this is the optimal number for logic-based tasks.

Mix Up Team Membership

If you leave the same people in the same teams, they'll feel their groups are more friendly, but at a price. Charlan Nemeth and Margaret Ormiston showed in a 2007 study that teams with a stable membership are less creative than newly formed teams.

Five Ways to Boost Group Creativity

The Importance of Unity

Multidisciplinary teams are especially effective, but without certain dynamics in place, they can risk breaking up into cliques. Based on a study of experts working within the U.K.'s National Health Service, Doris Fay and colleagues found teams that were more multidisciplinary came up with better-quality ideas than less multidisciplinary teams only when: all team members were committed to the same cause; everyone in the team felt listened to; the team reflected on its own effectiveness; and there was plenty of contact between team members.

Group Brainstorming Doesn't Work

Instead, team members should work on new ideas alone before pooling their suggestions together.

Introduce a New Team Member

You might not have enough personnel to keep refreshing the entire composition of your teams as suggested elsewhere. But in a 2005 study looking at three-person teams, Hoon-Seok Choi and Leigh Thompson showed that simply swapping one team member for a newcomer boosts the creativity of a group when compared to teams with a stable composition. Crucially, newcomers didn't just bring their own ideas to the table, they also boosted the creativity of the original two team members.

THE POWER OF MIMICS

We're all mimics. Have you ever noticed that when someone else yawns, you do too? You laugh, they laugh. They lean back, you lean back. Perhaps you even start using some of each other's catch-phrases, or parroting one another's accents. We all perform this social dance of mimicry to varying degrees. But why do we copy each other and what effect does it have?

Imitation Really Is the Sincerest Form of Flattery

In a study published in 2007, William Maddux at the INSEAD business school in Paris and colleagues arranged dozens of MBA students into pairs, with one person playing the role of employer while the other acted as job candidate. Their task was to negotiate the terms of employment. Crucially, half the students were told to mimic the mannerisms of their negotiation partner.

The effects of mimicry were impressive, especially considering no formal training was involved. Students who mimicked achieved more of their own negotiation aims, and what's more, their partners benefited too, tending to come away from the discussions with more gains than the students in pairs where no-one mimicked.

So what was going on? A further experiment established that student negotiators who mimicked were rated as more trustworthy than average, suggesting that may have been the key factor. However, the effects of mimicry go way beyond the perception of the mimicker. Dutch psychologist Rick van Baaren and his colleagues invited student participants to their lab to rate some adverts. While there,

half the students were mimicked by one of the researchers, an experience that positively biased the way these students behaved towards everyone, not just the person who mimicked them. For example, the mimicked students subsequently picked up more of the pens "accidentally" dropped by another of the researchers, and they also agreed to give more money to a charity than did the students who weren't mimicked.

It's almost as though there is something about being mimicked that puts us in a positive frame of mind, leading us to behave more altruistically. When what we see others doing is the same as what we're doing, it's easier for our brains to process, it's a fluent, rewarding experience. In fact, according to van Baaren, being mimicked is in some ways the default state, such that it has a negative effect on us when we're not mimicked. A study that looked at participants' brain activity when they either were or weren't being mimicked showed that not being mimicked was associated with increased activity in parts of the brain associated with negative emotions, including disgust!

Experts aren't sure why we tend to mimic each other, but from an evolutionary perspective, considering that humans have always been social animals, it certainly makes sense for us to engage in a behavior that will lead others to view us favorably. In this context, mimicry can be seen as a kind of social glue, helping build harmonious relationships. Furthermore, mimicry no doubt has advantages in terms of sheer survival value—if there is a threat to the group (for example, from a nearby wolf), it makes sense to copy what other people are doing (in this case, run and hide).

A Word of Warning

These findings may tempt you to try out mimicking in the real world, but before you do, beware the fact that the effects of mimicking completely backfire if people realize they are being mimicked. As we've discussed, mimicking is something that occurs naturally between interacting partners—if you deliberately try to imitate the body language of another person you may risk their noticing.

A possible way to reduce the likelihood of this happening is to introduce a delay before you copy another person's actions. So if they cross their legs, wait a few seconds before crossing your own. There doesn't seem to be any research yet on the optimum way to do this, but in studies where researchers have programmed a digital avatar (a computer-animated character) to mimic participants, they've tended to introduce a four-second delay in the mimicking. One study by Jeremy Bailenson and Nick Yee at Stanford University, for example, showed that an avatar that mimicked students with a four-second delay was rated as more persuasive than an avatar who didn't mimic.

CULTURE AND PERSPECTIVE-TAKING

The culture we're brought up in shapes the way we think about ourselves and others, even to the point of affecting the response of our brains to simple visual tasks. Most research in this area has focused on differences in perspective-taking between people raised in so-called collectivist cultures, such as China, Japan, and Korea, and those raised in more individualistic cultures, such as in North America and Western Europe.

Put crudely, in collectivist cultures people are encouraged to harmonize and adjust to others and to act appropriately. By contrast, people in individualistic cultures are encouraged to know what they want and to go out and get it.

These cultural differences can affect the extent to which individuals adopt the perspective of other people. When children reach the age of about four, they develop the ability to see things from other people's point of view. The effect of an individualistic culture is not to remove this ability, but rather to affect people's tendency to use it.

In a 2007 study by Shali Wu and Boaz Keysar at the University of Chicago, 20 non-Asian Americans and 20 Chinese people played a game that involved a researcher directing them to move objects in a shelf-like grid that could be viewed from both sides. Crucially, views of some of the boxes in the grid were blocked off from the researcher's side only, a fact that was apparent to the participants.

Boxing Clever

Wu and Keysar timed how long it took the participants to respond to simple instructions such as "Move the block up two squares," which were ambiguous only if the participants failed to take into account the researcher's perspective. For instance, there might have been two blocks, but only one visible to the researcher. Wu and Keysar found that the American participants were slower to respond than the Chinese, for example asking "Which block do you mean?"—thus revealing their failure to take the researcher's perspective.

Thinking of Others

In another study published the same year, Angela Leung at Singapore Management University and Dov Cohen at the University of Illinois at Urbana-Champaign showed vividly that when European Americans think about themselves they do so from a first-person perspective, whereas Asian Americans view themselves from a third-person perspective.

In one experiment, participants were told stories, their interpretation of which affected their understanding of subsequent ambiguous instructions. For example, one story involved a scenario in which the participant had gone to meet a friend at a skyscraper, but as they traveled in the elevator up to the 94th floor, their friend was in another elevator heading down to reception. Next, the same participants were given a map showing the city "Jackson" and asked to mark the location of the city "Jamestown" on it, which they were told, ambiguously, was the next city "after" Jackson on the north–south highway.

Yeung and Cohen found the Asian Americans were more likely to mark Jamestown as the next city south of Jackson, whereas the European Americans were more likely to mark it as the next city north. This corresponds with the idea that the Asian Americans had visualized the skyscraper story from their friend's perspective (their friend going down in the elevator biasing them to place Jamestown south), whereas the European Americans had visualized the story from their own perspective (their journey up the elevator biasing them to place Jamestown north).

How Long Is a Piece of String?

In 2008, Trey Hedden at Stanford University and his colleagues took this research a step further by looking at the effects of culture on brain activity. They showed that a simple visual task requiring an absolute judgment of line length led to increased activity in a swathe of brain areas in East Asian participants, compared with when they performed an almost identical task that required relative judgments. By contrast, the exact opposite pattern was found with European Americans—in their case it was the relative judgments that triggered a wave

of activity in their brains. Hedden and his team said that making absolute judgments is more effortful for people from collectivist cultures, thus requiring greater brain activity, whereas it is relative judgments that are the more demanding for people from individualistic cultures.

A PERSPECTIVE-TAKING THOUGHT EXPERIMENT

Imagine you're told: "Next Wednesday's meeting has been moved forward two days." What day do you think the meeting is now on? The answer may seem obvious, but people differ wildly in how they interpret this statement. If you see yourself as moving through time, you're likely to think the meeting has moved to Friday. However, if you see time as passing you by, you'll probably think it's on Monday.

PERSONAL RELATIONSHIPS

We're social animals and close relationships are essential to our mental well-being. There's even research showing that married people live longer than singles. Robert Kaplan and Richard Kronick at the University of California checked on the marital status of tens of thousands of people in 1989 and then looked to see who was still alive in 1997. Compared with married people, singles were far more likely to have died during that time, especially if they had never been married.

Meanwhile, research by Constantine Sedikides at Southampton University has shown that merely thinking about people who are close to us can have protective effects on our mental well-being. Participants whom Sedikides asked to think about an intimate other were subsequently more receptive to being told by researchers about weaknesses in their own mental abilities, presumably because thinking about a loved one had acted as a shield for their self-esteem. Here are five tips for a healthy relationship

Be Generous With Your Support

Providing ample, unconditional support to your partner won't make them needy, rather it will lead them toward greater independence and self-sufficiency—a finding psychologist Brooke Feeney of Carnegie Mellon University has dubbed the "dependency paradox." One study of 165 married couples found that husbands and wives who received plenty of unconditional support from their partners were more likely to have achieved a stated goal six months later, and to report being self-sufficient and feeling secure.

Keep In Touch

There are times in life when it can be difficult to maintain our closest friendships. Psychologists Debra Oswald and Eddie Clark studied 137 students who were making their transition from school to university. By the following Spring, only 55 percent of them still considered their best friend from school to be their closest friend. Which friendships survived? Oswald and Clark found that geographical distance was irrelevant. Friendship survival depended on frequent phone contact, the sharing of private thoughts, and being cheerful and upbeat when together. What's more, the students who remained close to their best friend from school were less likely to complain of loneliness during their first year at university.

Write About Your Relationship

Writing about your relationship could increase its longevity, according to a study by Richard Slatcher and James Pennebaker at the University of Texas at Austin. Of 86 heterosexual undergrads, Slatcher and Pennebaker asked half to write about their romantic relationship for 20 minutes a day for three days. The other half wrote about their daily activities. Three months later, 77 percent of the students who'd written about their relationship were still with the same partner, compared with just 52 percent of the students who'd written about their activities. Analysis of instant messaging communication between the students and their partners showed that writing about a relationship led couples to use more positive emotional words when communicating with each other.

Keep Things Equal

According to social exchange theory, if one partner in a relationship perceives that they are receiving less than they are giving, in terms of a range of factors including love, money, status, and sex, then prospects for the future of the relationship won't be good. Susan Sprecher at Illinois State University followed the progress of 101 student couples for nearly five years. She found that participants who felt they gave more than they received tended to report feeling less satisfied and less committed to their relationship, and there was a greater likelihood of the relationship ending. However, Sprecher cautioned that the direction of causality wasn't always clear. In some cases it may be that a lack of relationship satisfaction and commitment leads people to feel that they are receiving less from a relationship than they are giving.

Speak Positively to Each Other

Marriage expert John Gottman, director of the Relationship Research Institute in Seattle, Washington, has found that he can predict the likelihood of marriages lasting with an extraordinary degree of accuracy, based purely on an analysis of the way that couples talk to each other. Couples were video-taped as they discussed an issue they disagreed on, or as they discussed their past. Among couples whose relationships survived over the ensuing three years, there was a 5:1 ratio of positive statements to negative statements. By contrast, for couples whose relationships didn't last, the ratio was approximately 1:1.

Antonio Damasio

Antonio Damasio is an influential neurologist and neuroscientist, perhaps best known for his popular books about the biological basis of consciousness and the emotions. These include *The Feeling of What Happens*, which was named one of the top ten books of 2001 by the *New York Times*, and *Descartes' Error*, both translated in over 30 languages.

Damasio was born in Lisbon, studied medicine at the University of Lisbon (MD, 1969), and completed his Ph.D. in 1974. Today, Damasio is "David Domsife Professor of Neuroscience" and Director of the Brain and Creativity Institute at the University of Southern California. He has earned countless prizes including the Prince of Asturias Award for Technical and Scientific Research in 2005, and is a member of the Institute of Medicine of the National Academy of Sciences.

Damasio and his wife Hanna Damasio (a respected neuroscientist in her own right) study brain-damaged patients, and use brain-imaging techniques in an attempt to understand the neurological basis of the self, the emotions, and decision-making. Damasio believes a core sense of self arises from our brain's representation of the body, including its internal states as it is modified by engagement with an object—perceived or imagined—leading us to experience a "feeling of what happens." Autobiographical details, which are dependent on memory systems, form the basis of what Damasio calls our "extended self."

It is Damasio's hope that work on the biological bases of emotions and decision-making can be brought together with work at other levels of investigation to reach a solution to human conflict, and to solve the mystery of consciousness.

Moral Decision-Making

Damasio has also shown the role played by emotions in our moral decision-making. Consider the dilemma of whether or not you as a hostage would be prepared to kill another hostage in return for the release of yourself and eight children. What would you do? Most people recoil from the prospect of deliberately killing another, so choose instead to sacrifice the freedom of the majority for the life of that person. By contrast, patients with damage to the ventromedial prefrontal cortex (who lack emotions) make more utilitarian choices in these kinds of situations—favoring killing one person for the benefit of the majority. However, when it comes to less personal moral choices, these patients make the same choices as healthy people.

TEST OUT THE SOMATIC-MARKER HYPOTHESIS

Experts used to think of decision-making as being a purely rational process, but one of Damasio's best-known theories is the Somatic Marker hypothesis, which outlines the key role played by emotions in decision-making.

One way Damasio has tested his somatic-marker theory is by using a gambling task which is designed to capture in a simple test the rewards, punishments, and uncertainty of life. You can try this out on your friends. First you need to create a set of about 100 cards, which must be arranged into four piles. Cards in piles A and B carry rewards of $100 each, but one in every ten cards has a penalty of $1,250. Cards in piles C and D have rewards of just $50, with one $250 penalty card in every ten. You need to get all the cards and piles arranged appropriately, without giving away any of these details to your friends. Then ask a friend to take one card at a time from any of the piles, with the aim to accumulate as much money as possible in 50 cards. Watch how they play and remember to keep a score of their earnings if you want to compare the performance of your different friends.

At first, your friend won't know what to expect and will probably be drawn to the piles that carry the higher rewards. But as they play on, you should see that they instinctively start to take more cards from piles C and D, which is the shrewd strategy for earning more money. Antonio Damasio showed that emotions play a key role in successful performance at this task. Patients with damage to the ventromedial prefrontal cortex, who have normal intelligence but impaired emotions, continue taking from piles A and B—a behavior that reflects their abysmal decision-making in real life. Problem gamblers also show this pattern.

Damasio also measured the emotional response (based on the sweatiness of their fingers) of healthy people as they played the game. Even before they'd made the wise move to take cards consistently from piles C and D, Damasio found these participants showed an emotional response before picking up cards from the disadvantageous piles. This suggests it is our emotional response to the cards that guides our decision-making, even before we fully realize it.

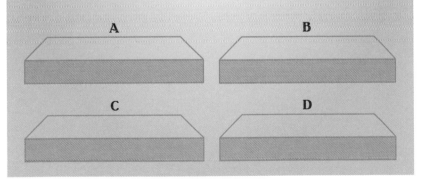

MINDBLINDNESS

Central to successful socializing is our ability to represent to ourselves the perspective of other people—to imagine ourselves in their shoes. Psychologists call this having a "Theory of Mind" because, literally, it is about forming theories of other people's mental states. However, in children and adults with autism (from the Greek autos, meaning self) or Asperger's Syndrome, this ability is severely impaired, leading to what some experts have dubbed "Mindblindness."

There are several ways this manifests as the child with autism grows up. For example, a typical 14-month-old toddler will follow another person's gaze to see what they are looking at, whereas the child with autism or Asperger's will do this far less. A typical nine-year-old will understand when a social faux pas has occurred—those instances when someone has done something embarrassing or that might upset or offend others. By contrast, children of that age, and even adults, who have autism or Asperger's, find it difficult to recognize when these kinds of social transgressions have occurred.

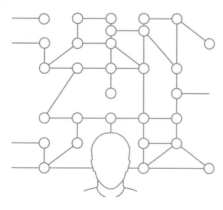

Whereas early theories about autism dwelt on these social deficits, more contemporary theories recognize another feature of the condition, which is that people with autism tend to be very good at understanding and analyzing systems, such as syntax, weather patterns, or calendars. The autism expert Simon Baron-Cohen has developed a theory which is based on understanding this mixture of poor empathizing with superior systematizing. His approach recognizes that we all vary on these dimensions, and that autism merely represents an extreme end of a normal continuum.

Autistic Pride

You may have heard of autistic savants—people with autism who, alongside their difficulties, have a rare, extreme talent, such as for drawing in intricate, beautiful detail, or for calculating instantly what day a given date falls on. However, a growing movement is recognizing the latent abilities of all people with autism and Asperger's, not just the savants. This perspective argues that the autistic brain doesn't have anything wrong with it, it's just different. Advocates believe it is wrong for society to

ARE YOU AN EMPATHIZER OR SYSTEMATIZER?

1. I prefer to speak to people in person rather than emailing. TRUE/FALSE

2. When I listen to music, I enjoy recognizing the way it is structured. TRUE/FALSE

3. I find it hard to predict how people will feel in a given situation. TRUE/FALSE

4. If I were buying a mobile phone, I wouldn't be interested in the details of how it works. TRUE/FALSE

5. If someone starts to get upset, it can make me get upset too. TRUE/FALSE

6. I have my clothes organized carefully according to type. TRUE/FALSE

7. I don't like to think of animals suffering. TRUE/FALSE

8. I'm not keen on fixed routines or plans. TRUE/FALSE

9. I've been told before that I am sometimes insensitive, but I can't see why. TRUE/FALSE

10. Bus and train timetables are easy to understand. TRUE/FALSE

11. I can usually tell how other people are feeling. TRUE/FALSE

12. I'm not bothered with the "small print." TRUE/FALSE

These statements are inspired by items from the Empathizing Quotient and Systematizing Quotient developed by the Autism Research Centre in Cambridge, England.

seek a "cure" for autism; instead they say we should celebrate the "neuro-diversity" between individuals.

Famous Autists

There are some people in the world whose remarkable success and expertise appears related to the unusual skills they have by virtue of being autistic or having Asperger's. Examples of such people include the talented British mathematician Richard Borcherds, winner of the prestigious Fields Medal; and the well-known American expert on animal behavior Temple Grandin.

SCORING

Empathising: Score a point each time you answer true to items 1,5,7,11, and each time you answer false to 3,9. The more points you scored, the more of an empathizer you are.

Systematizing: Score a point each time you answer true to items 2,6,10 and each time you answer false to 4,8, and 12. The more points you score, the more of a systematizer you are. People with autism and Asperger's tend to score very high on systematizing and very low on empathizing. There are also sex differences: men tend to score higher on the systematizing scale but lower on the empathizing scale relative to women. This is consistent with the far higher prevalence of autism (4:1) and Asperger's (9:1) among men relative to women, which has led Simon Baron-Cohen to propose that autism represents an extreme form of the male brain.

Social Self

THE PROBLEM:

You're a hotel manager on a mission to improve the green credentials of your business. One of the most profligate activities in your hotel is the laundry. As of today you've decided to embark on an initiative to encourage more of your guests to re-use their towels. What's the most effective message you can place in hotel bathrooms to achieve this change in behavior?

THE METHOD:

Most hotels have messages in the bathrooms saying something about their commitment to the planet, and inviting guests to help out by replacing their towels on the rail. A related strategy is to give statistics on the amount of water and detergent that's used in the business of providing daily clean towels, presumably in the hope of shocking guests into realising the waste that's involved in providing them with a freshly laundered towel each day.

What these messages fail to exploit effectively is the power of what's called "social norms." This term describes the fact that we tend to copy how we believe other people behave. And when it comes to any kind of unhealthy or antisocial activity, individuals often console themselves that most other people indulge in the same way.

Standard hotel bathroom messages actually invoke the power of social norms in a way that backfires. By spreading information about all the waste that's involved in towel washing, new guests are given the message that it's incredibly common for other guests to put their towels in the laundry each day, which will only encourage the new guests to follow suit.

A great deal of persuasion research has shown that, rather than providing shocking statistics about an unwanted behavior, it's more effective to correct the misperception about the prevalence of that behavior. That way, people lose one of their main excuses for their own behavior, and many feel an automatic instinct to follow the herd in behaving in a more socially desirable fashion.

Take the example of binge-drinking by students at university. Research has shown that many students have an exaggerated sense of how many of their peers binge drink. Informing them about how few of their fellow students really do overindulge has been shown to be far more effective at reducing campus binge-drinking than publishing shock-style adverts about how many students do binge drink.

THE SOLUTION:

The most effective message you can leave in your hotel bathrooms will invoke the power of social norms. By giving your guests the impression that most other people staying in the hotel re-use their towels, you will encourage them to follow suit.

This approach was put to the test in a 2008 study by Noah Goldstein and his colleagues at the University of Chicago Graduate School of Business. The researchers placed one of two kinds of message in the bathrooms of a hotel in the US Southwest: one of them simply implored guests to help protect the environment by re-using their towels more often; the other invited guests to join other guests in helping the environment, and gave the key statistic that "almost 75 percent of guests" already did their bit by re-using their towels.

Over the course of their stay, the guests in this study who received the social norms message were more likely to re-use their towels (44.1 percent of them did so compared with 35.1 percent of guests who received the standard message). Further research has shown that this kind of message is even more effective if it provides data showing that most guests staying in *that exact* room choose to re-use their towels, and if the data is combined with a broader statement about the high number of guests who have expressed their concerns about the environment and the importance of conserving energy.

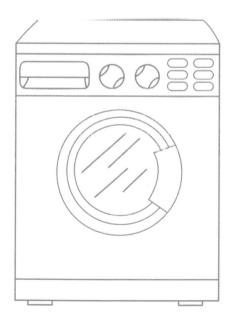

6

Personality

For over a hundred years psychologists have been fascinated with how best to categorize and describe the different types of person based on their enduring behavioral and emotional characteristics. We'll look at the tests they use and the emerging consensus on the different types of personality trait. Also: why do some people make great leaders, and what happens when personality goes awry?

PROJECTIVE TESTS

Personality is one of those concepts that we're always referring to in everyday conversation, yet which we seldom stop to consider in any depth. On the one hand, we're all unique, so what's the point of saying anything about Joe Bloggs's personality beyond the fact that his character is like, well, Joe Bloggs?

On the other hand, there are certain situations—imagine having been starving and then finally getting something to eat—in which we'd presumably all respond in pretty much the same way, with sighs of relief and grunts of satisfaction. From this perspective, Joe Bloggs's personality, like the rest of us, is simply human. Usually, therefore, when we talk about someone's personality, we're navigating between these extremes: we're saying something interesting about the enduring ways in which this person is similar to some people, and yet different from others. More on this in the Big Five Personality Factors (see pages 116–17).

Measuring Personality

A problem with measuring people's personality is that if you ask someone about themselves, they're likely to tell you what they think you want to hear: "Yes, I'm a caring person," "No, I never get jealous." It's to overcome these "issues of social desirability," as they're known, that some psychologists advocate the use of projective tests such as the famous Rorschach Inkblot Test and the Thematic Apperception Test (TAT). The idea with these open-ended tests is that we can't help but project something of who we are in the way that we interpret ambiguous pictures.

It must be stated that these projective tests are controversial. The whole point of psychology is that it applies the objective scrutiny of science to human nature. For this reason, contemporary psychology dictates that effective tests must be both reliable and valid. Reliability refers to how similar scores on the test will be with repeated testing by the same individual, or with repeated scoring by different markers. Individuals who are matched on whatever is being measured should also score similarly. Validity refers to whether the test measures what it claims to be measuring.

Critics of the Rorschach and TAT claim that they are lacking on both these criteria. The same participant, they say, is likely to respond in wildly different ways on repeated testing, and two different judges are likely to score their answers in different ways. And arguably, it's not always clear what the tests are actually measuring, so in that sense they lack validity. Having said all that, many psychologists, especially in the United States, do still endorse these tests and they would disagree that the tests lack reliability and validity. Indeed, in the United States the tests are still used by some psychologists acting as expert court witnesses, for example in custody cases.

The Rorschach Test

Devised by the eponymous Swiss psychiatrist Hermann Rorschach, the ink-blot test involves the participant looking at ten symmetrical ink-blots and describing what they see. Participants' responses to each blot are traditionally scored according to three factors: the parts of the inkblot that they focus on; the shape, form, color, and perceived movement that they describe; and the content that they interpret the blot as showing, especially in terms of the presence of human, animal, or anatomical shapes. The image above shows one of the original blots used by Rorschach. What do you see?

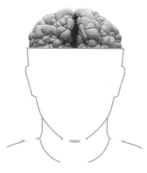

The Thematic Apperception Test

Devised by the Harvard psychologist Henry Murray in the 1930s, this test involves the participant looking at a series of deliberately ambiguous line drawings showing one or more people in various situations. For example, one of the original drawings shows a woman lying in bed with her eyes closed, while a man stands nearby covering his face with his arm. It's not at all clear whether the woman is asleep, ill, or even dead. The man, meanwhile, could be upset, relieved, or merely stretching. The participants' task is to tell the story of what is happening before, during, and after the scene. The psychologist will make inferences about the participant based on these stories. So in the aforementioned example, a story involving murder may be taken to reveal hostility toward women, while a story involving a partner who is sick or who has died could be taken to reveal sympathy and respect toward women. You can do an internet search for "thematic apperception test" to locate some of the original TAT pictures.

THE BIG FIVE PERSONALITY FACTORS

As discussed in the preceding pages, personality is about describing those enduring ways in which a person is similar to some people yet different from others. If you consider the number of words we have for describing each other—lively, shy, considerate, reckless, humble, proud, arrogant, brave… the list goes on and on—then you'll soon realize what a daunting task it has been for psychology to find a scientific way to capture the essence of what someone is like.

The science of personality isn't just about description, it's also about prediction—someone's personality can impact on a range of outcomes, anything from the likely success of their marriage to their probable longevity.

The Key Factors of You

Various philosophers and psychologists have proposed the key factors which they think capture personality in a parsimonious yet comprehensive way. For example, Hans Eysenck argued for the existence of two personality dimensions: extraversion vs. introversion and neuroticism vs. stability. A third dimension, psychoticism vs. socialization, was added to his theory later. Raymond Cattell meanwhile proposed that there are 16 factors underlying personality: warmth, reasoning, emotional stability, dominance, to name just a few.

After years of research and with the help of a statistical technique called factor analysis, most psychologists now agree there are five main traits underlying personality, known as the Big Five Factors. These have been arrived at by stripping out all the redundancy in the way that we describe people. For example, take the following personality traits: creative, imaginative, eccentric. Research shows that if a person scores high on one of these traits, then they're likely to score high on the other two. In other words, these three traits are really all describing the more fundamental attribute that psychologists call "Openness." The other four Big Factors are: Extraversion (how outgoing vs. quiet a person is), Neuroticism (how prone to worry vs. stable), Conscientiousness (how diligent vs. reckless), and Agreeableness (how trusting vs. hostile).

MEASURE YOUR PERSONALITY

The following test and its interpretation are inspired by the Newcastle Personality Assessor. For the next 12 statements, give yourself a score from 1 (not me at all) to 5 (that's exactly what I'm like).

1. I put other people's interests first.
2. My house/bedroom is a bit of a mess (reverse score).
3. I often feel down.
4. I plan ahead.
5. I'm musical, artistic, and/or enjoy writing.
6. I like throwing parties or arranging nights out.
7. I feel for other people if they get upset.
8. I often dwell on the meaning of life.
9. I enjoy meeting new people.
10. I often dread things.
11. I'm interested in words.
12. I don't have any qualms about insulting people (reverse score).

Our scores on the five factors are determined by a mixture of genetics and early life experiences. Daniel Nettle at the University of Newcastle has said that the Big Five Factors can be viewed as shorthand for the way that a person is wired up. He says the factors are akin to a series of thermostats, with people differing in the thresholds at which they are knocked into a given state, such as anxiety or arousal, depending on the situation.

How Stable is Personality?

Psychologists disagree about this. The notion that personality is fixed, come what may, has been dubbed the "fundamental attribution error" by critics who believe situations play a powerful role in the way that we behave. Both extremes of the argument can be empowering or disheartening depending on how you interpret them.

The idea that personality is fixed is reassuring in the sense that it suggests we will stay true to ourselves, no matter what life throws at us. On the other hand, we might not like ourselves much, and this fixed view of personality implies that we're stuck the way we are without any capacity for change. So to people who dream of change, the strong situationist approach to personality is appealing, arguing as it does that we can all become whoever we want to be, given the right circumstances.

SCORING

Extraversion: Add your points for 9 and 6.
Neuroticism: Items 3 and 10.
Conscientiousness: Items 4 and 2.
Agreeableness: Items 1, 7 and 12.
Openness: Items 5, 8, 11.
Remember to reverse-score items 2 and 12.

How Do You Size Up?

This is extremely crude, but for Extraversion, Neuroticism, and Conscientiousness, 4 or below is a low score; 5 or 6 is medium; and 7 and above is high. For Agreeableness, 9 or less is a low score for men, 14 and 15 are high, in between is medium. For women 11 or fewer is low, 14 and 15 are high, in between is medium. For openness, 8 or less is low, 13 or above is high, the rest are medium.

LEADERSHIP MATERIAL

History is littered with both inspiring (Winston Churchill, Joan of Arc) and notorious leaders (Adolf Hitler, Pol Pot), and so perhaps it is no surprise that early psychological theories about leadership dwelt on the kind of person who makes an influential leader. However, this "great man" approach has since fallen out of favor as psychologists have recognized that what makes a good leader varies with the situation and with the group that is being led.

According to the psychologists Stephen Reicher, Alexander Haslam, and Michael Platow, effective leaders are people who are seen to represent the interests of their followers. Members of a coherent group will have a shared identity with shared goals, and their leader, if effective, will come to be seen as encapsulating that identity and as coordinating efforts to reach those goals. However, it is a dynamic process, so that the most effective leaders will not just represent the identity of their group, they will also shape it.

Taking this perspective on leadership generates predictions which the latest research appears to support. For example, one experiment showed that the efforts of team members diminished as their leader's pay increased up to triple of what they were being paid. That is presumably because followers struggle to identify with a leader who they perceive is not in the same boat as them. Some of history's recent leaders have heeded this lesson. Just think of Yasser Arafat in his headscarf, George W. Bush in his cowboy hat and jeans, or Ghandi in his villager's dress—in each case these leaders were saying to their followers, "I am just like you."

FIVE SURPRISING FINDINGS ABOUT LEADERSHIP

1. Appearances seem to matter, at least when it comes to the chief executives of companies in America. Nicholas Rule and Nalini Ambady asked 100 students to rate the appearance of 50 faces. Unbeknown to the students, these were the faces of chief execs of the most and least profitable companies on the Fortune 500 website. The leaders of the most profitable companies were rated as more competent, dominant, and mature than the leaders of the least profitable companies. It's not clear whether working for a certain type of company influences the appearance of its chief exec; whether having a chief exec with a certain kind of face affects the fortunes of his/her company; or whether successful vs. unsuccessful companies differ in the kind of looks they go for in their chief executives.

2. A strong leader isn't always a good thing. An investigation of several Chinese companies found that in those organizations with a good customer service ethos, strong team leaders had a negligible effect on external customer service, while actually lowering internal customer service (contact between colleagues). What could have been going on? According to Harry Hui and colleagues it's possible the strong leaders were out of sync with their organization's broader service climate. For example, the company may prescribe standardized ways of dealing with customers, while the strong leader may preach innovation.

3. Effective leadership is sometimes associated with a hesitant speaking style. Fifty-four participants rated the leadership potential of a fictitious man called Richard, based on one of two versions of a telephone conversation. In one version he seemed assertive and confident; in the other he spoke with doubt and hesitation. Those participants who were told that Richard was being considered for a company that valued employees' ability to work alone rated him as a more suitable leader if they'd heard the conversation in which he was confident. By contrast, the participants told the company favored cooperation among staff rated Richard as a better potential leader if they'd read the hesitant telephone conversation.

4. It helps to be the first-born. Studies have found that first-born children are over-represented among leaders of countries around the world. A study in 2003 by Rudy Andeweg and Steef Van Den Berg found that only children are also over-represented among leaders, thus suggesting that the benefit of being a first-born has something to do with all that parental attention.

5. It may help to have hair. America hasn't had a bald president since Dwight D. Eisenhower. William Hague and Iain Duncan-Smith, both strikingly bald, became the first and second Conservative leaders, respectively, to fail to become British Prime Minister since Austen Chamberlain in the early 1920s.

PERFECTIONIST PERSONALITIES

Do you often experience the nagging feeling that you could have done better? Do you find that you are always criticizing yourself? If so, it sounds like you may well have a perfectionist personality.

Being a perfectionist is a double-edged sword—in moderation it is associated with high attainment, but taken to extremes it can lead to mental health problems. People with an extremely perfectionist personality are at increased risk of developing anxiety disorders such as obsessive-compulsive disorder, eating disorders like anorexia, and even committing suicide.

Whether perfectionism leads to problems usually depends on other aspects of a person's personality. For example, setting high standards for oneself can be a good thing, and many high achievers of course do just that, but if someone can't cope with not reaching those high standards then that's when problems can occur.

A study carried out by British Psychologists Rory O'Connor and Daryl O'Connor, meanwhile, found that perfectionist students were at increased risk of psychological distress only if they also tended to deal with problems by avoiding them. Neither avoidant coping nor perfectionism were problematic on their own.

What is Obsessive-Compulsive Disorder?

One mental health problem with which excessive perfectionism is strongly associated is obsessive-compulsive disorder (OCD). People with OCD experience nagging obsessive thoughts, such as about

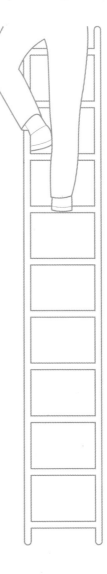

ARE YOU A MAXIMIZER OR A SATISFICER?

According to Barry Schwartz at Swarthmore College, where one kind of perfectionist who is particularly prone to problems is the "maximizer." Maximizers are characterized by their determination always to make the best choice—which in reality of course is an impossible task. There's always one more shop to look in, one more restaurant to try. Satisficers on the other hand are better equipped to deal with the explosion of choices that we face in the modern world. The satisficer is happy to settle for what is good enough, without feeling any pressure to seek out the very best.

The following test is inspired by Schwartz's own maximization scale. For each of the following eight items, give yourself a score from 1 (completely disagree) to 7 (completely agree).

1. I'm always imagining what a different kind of life from my own could be like.

2. I can't stand those lists you get in magazines and on TV shows in which they count down the best of this of the best of that.

3. I spend ages shopping because I like to compare the same product between stores.

4. I rarely look at job adverts—I'm content with the job I've got.

5. When I'm confronted with a choice, I like to consider all the options available to me, even those that aren't on the table.

6. I'm quick at writing emails and mobile phone texts because I rarely worry about how I've phrased things.

7. When I'm watching a TV show, I often find myself wondering if I'm missing something better on another channel.

8. When I met my partner I knew they were the one for me or I don't expect to work through loads of relationships before finding my perfect match.

cleanliness or safety, which they are only able to relieve by performing certain compulsions. These compulsions normally take the form of repeated washing or checking. The condition becomes problematic when it starts interfering with everyday life.

Unlike problem gamblers or drinkers who say they find their betting or drinking enjoyable (at least at the outset of their addiction), people with OCD derive no pleasure from their compulsions.

SCORING

Subtract your points for items 2, 4, 6, and 8 from your points for items 1, 3, 5, and 7. If you're left with a positive score, then you're more of a maximizer than a satisficer, whereas if you're left with a negative score, you're more of a satisficer. According to Barry Schwartz, maximizers should watch out—the combination of your mentality with the abundance of choice in the modern Western world is likely to lead you to frustration and unhappiness.

MULTIPLE PERSONALITIES

We've all heard of Dr. Jekyll and Mr. Hyde, but can people really have more than one personality? It's incredibly rare, but yes, there are indeed reports of people having multiple alter egos—a condition that was known as multiple personality disorder, but which today is referred to as dissociative identity disorder (DID).

Perhaps the best known case is that of Sibyl, who in the 1970s was reported to possess 16 different personalities. Her story was first told in a book by journalist Flora Schreiber and has since been made into a mini-series (in 1976) and a film (in 2007). Another case made famous in the '50s was Eve, who eventually claimed 22 different alter egos, and whose story was also turned into a film.

The diagnosis of DID is extremely controversial, not least because it is difficult to ascertain how much a person with the condition is acting or responding to suggestion. It doesn't help that alter egos have often been identified under hypnosis. What's more, the number of reported cases has tended to rise and fall dramatically depending on the profile of the condition, with an "epidemic" having occurred in the '80s and '90s when the condition reached its highest profile.

Diagnosing Multiple Personalities

Today DID is recognized as one of a cluster of psychiatric conditions, alongside depersonalization disorder (feeling that you are no longer real), dissociative fugue (forgetting who you are and your life story), and dissociative amnesia (forgetting certain past experiences in your life). A diagnosis

of these conditions is made only in the absence of a clear organic cause, such as brain injury or disease. The preference of contemporary psychiatry has been to shift the emphasis away from the idea of multiple personalities, to focus more on the apparent breakdown in consciousness and memory seen in all these patients, hence the association of DID with fugue states and depersonalization.

A popular theory is that multiple personalities and other forms of dissociation emerge as a way of coping with extreme and continuous trauma, especially in childhood. This would appear to make some intuitive sense. For example, in some patients only one or some of their personalities will have access to memories of the trauma they claim to have experienced in childhood, while the other personalities will appear to be protected from the pain of these recalled experiences. However, these observations are based almost entirely on the self-report of patients and there are clear problems with suggestibility in therapy.

On balance, in very rare circumstances, some form of personality splitting probably can occur and is probably related in some way to experiencing trauma. In a wide-ranging review published in 2005, an

Psychology: Adventures in Perception and Personality

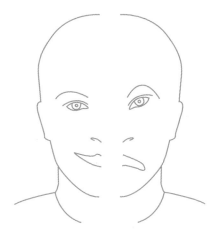

expert on dissociative disorders, John Kihlstrom at the University of California, concluded that: "As complex as they surely are, they deserve to be studied in a spirit of open inquiry that avoids both the excessive credulity of the enthusiast and the dismissal of the determined skeptic." To date there has been very little experimental study of people with apparent multiple personalities—for example, to see how the different personalities score on established personality tests.

THOUGHT EXPERIMENT: LEGAL ISSUES

The dissociative disorders raise all sorts of difficulties when it comes to judging criminal responsibility. For example, imagine a suspect in court has been diagnosed by a psychiatrist as having DID, with multiple personalities. What if the suspect claims that their dominant, host personality did not commit the crime; that the offender was one of their other personalities? Should the entire person be held accountable? Or consider the case of fugue states, in which the person has forgotten who they are. Should convicted criminals be held just as culpable even if they have

no recollection of the crimes they committed? Not only can these be awkward issues, but of course such scenarios also raise the suspicion of malingering. This happened in the real-life case of the "Hillside Strangler" Kenneth Bianchi, who, with his cousin, was charged with the murder of several women in 1970s Los Angeles. Bianchi claimed to have multiple personality disorder and that one of his alter egos had committed the murders, but court psychologists decided he was malingering, and he was sentenced to life imprisonment.

DISORDERED PERSONALITIES

People diagnosed with a personality disorder have extreme character traits that cause them to find life difficult, so that they, and often those close to them, suffer as a result.

There are ten forms of personality disorder listed in the current version of psychiatry's diagnostic bible, *The Diagnostic and Statistical Manual, IV*. These are: schizoid, schizotypal, paranoid (known collectively as the odd/eccentric cluster); antisocial, borderline, histrionic, narcissistic (the dramatic/erratic cluster); and avoidant, dependent, and obsessive-compulsive (the anxious/avoidant cluster).

The whole notion of personality disorders has proved to be extremely controversial. Critics have asked how it can make any sense to label someone with a personality disorder if experts can't even agree on what exactly personality is or how to measure it. And anyway, these critics add, isn't there a large amount of subjectivity involved?

Indeed, you can imagine that a Hollywood actor teleported to an English country village might well be judged by locals to be disconcertingly histrionic and narcissistic. Likewise, a dedicated trader on Wall Street might, if transported to an Amsterdam café, be perceived as worryingly obsessive. The scientific soundness of the personality disorder concept is further undermined by the fact that the same person will often meet the diagnostic criteria for several different types of personality disorder.

Nonetheless, despite these concerns, the consensus among the mental health professions is that personality disorders do exist. There can be little doubt that there are people in the world who struggle persistently with life, at least in part because of their pervasive personality traits. For these individuals, identifying that they have a personality disorder can be a crucial first step on the path to helping them. Indeed, despite the widespread belief to the contrary, experts now state emphatically that personality disorders can be treated.

How Common Is It?

According to a recent report published by the British Psychological Society, around 10 percent of the population have a personality disorder. Perhaps unsurprisingly, rates of personality disorder are far higher among psychiatric inpatients and outpatients, and are most prevalent of all among prison inmates, where some studies have reported rates as high as 70 percent.

What's the Cause?

Some aspects of our personality are doubtless inherited, but we're also shaped by our upbringing and by our ongoing circumstances and experiences. Research shows that physical and sexual abuse in childhood can predispose people toward developing a personality disorder, as can parental alcoholism and parents' failure to supervise or discipline their children.

What is Someone with a Personality Disorder Like?

It's all very well reading about the notion of a personality disorder, but what is someone with this diagnosis really like? Hopefully these fictional examples will help explain.

Sally (avoidant personality) looked set for a successful academic career despite her life-long shyness and introversion. However, she left her research position after claiming she felt uncomfortable in meetings and hated delivering presentations. Soon she started staying in on Fridays, instead of going to the pub with her husband as had been their routine. After initially claiming she was fine, Sally saw her physician, saying her shyness had become debilitating. Her physician referred her to a specialist mental-health team for further assessment and help.

Christopher (antisocial personality) was first charged with a criminal offence at the age of 13 after stealing a car. He spent his teenage years in and out of care, getting into fights, and committing acts of vandalism and theft. As a young adult, he was soon jailed following his serious violent assault on a parking warden. Staff in jail say he shows no remorse and dominates any group therapy sessions.

As well as demonstrating the kinds of people who are likely to be diagnosed with a personality disorder, these examples also show why the concept can be contentious. Does Sally really have a personality disorder that needs treating, or is she just a very shy person? Does Christopher have a personality disorder or is he just a "nasty piece of work?" This is an issue that is also touched upon in the box above.

MAD OR BAD?

As with dissociative identify disorder (see pages 122–23), the notion of personality disorders poses a quandary for the judicial system. Put simply, if someone with a personality disorder commits a crime, are they mad or bad?

This issue was thrust into the spotlight in the U.K. in 2005 when the 19-year-old Brian Blackwell was jailed for life for the brutal killing of both his parents. Blackwell had lived a fantasist's life, including convincing his girlfriend that he was a professional tennis player. After his arrest he was diagnosed with narcissistic personality disorder and he subsequently pleaded guilty to two counts of manslaughter on the basis of diminished responsibility. But does that label really explain why Blackwell behaved the way he did, or is it just a description?

At the time, the press certainly reported on the case as if Blackwell's diagnosis explained his behavior. The Telegraph newspaper wrote that: "The illness made Blackwell obsessed with fantasies of unlimited success, power and brilliance." The BBC said that Blackwell's condition "made him feel entitled to unlimited success in all areas of his life, he was a slave to his fantasy view of himself as brilliant and untouchable."

Sigmund Freud

Sigmund Freud, the grandfather of psychoanalysis, started out as a hard-nosed scientist and medic. After qualifying in medicine from the University of Vienna in 1881, he went on to study the reproductive organs of the eel, his first scientific paper being entitled: "Observations on the Form and the Finer Structure of the Lobular Organs of the Eel, Organs Considered to be Testes."

Freud also published early works on aphasia (loss of language due to brain injury) and wrote a landmark paper on the psychological properties of cocaine, based largely on self-experimentation. However, it wasn't until he studied under the celebrated neurologist Jean-Martin Charcot at the world-famous Salpêtrière Hospital in Paris, that Freud's metamorphosis into a psychologist and therapist really took off.

In Paris, Freud met patients diagnosed with hysteria—that is, the manifestation of ostensibly physical symptoms in the absence of any discernible organic cause. From this moment Freud set out to develop a comprehensive theory of the mind. Groundbreaking publications followed, including *The Interpretation of Dreams* and *Beyond the Pleasure Principle*. Thanks to Freud, the psychoanalytic movement was born. Today the man's influence can be felt beyond psychology, in literature, painting, and anthropology. Freud would end his days in London, having fled the Nazi occupation of Austria.

Echoes of Freud in Modern Neuroscience

Freud's work is often dismissed as a form of "pre-science," relying as it did on his detailed investigations of single case studies, rather than on the repeated, controlled testing of participant groups, of the kind performed in modern psychology. Moreover, Freud's proposal that the mind is made up of an id, ego, and super-ego is today viewed by many as seriously outdated—nothing more than superficial reification. By contrast, other experts recognize that Freud would have been the first to seek a biological basis for his psychological musings, were he to have had access to our modern techniques. What's more, many psychologists see echoes of Freud's ideas in new psychological findings.

Anosognosia

Freud suggested that we have defense mechanisms which protect us from unacceptable or unbearable truths. Modern-day neurologists have identified a condition, observed among some neurological patients, known as anosognosia, which strongly resembles these kinds of defense mechanisms. Patients with anosognosia, who have damage to the right parietal region of their brains, appear to be in complete denial about their disabilities. For example, a woman with a paralyzed arm will refuse to accept there is anything wrong with it, and will even concoct elaborate excuses for why she isn't using her afflicted limb.

Dreams as Wish Fulfillment

Freud said that when we're asleep, the base desires of the id are given more freedom as the ego and superego are at rest. This situation manifests as dreams, which can represent our true wishes in all their unashamed glory. Early neuroscience findings debunked this idea as they suggested dreams are associated with the stage of sleep known as Rapid Eye Movement (REM) sleep, which is itself triggered by processes in the brain stem, not by brain areas involved with motivation. More recent findings, however, have shown that dreaming is not confined to REM sleep and that frontal parts of the brain involved in motivation do indeed play a part in the production of our nocturnal adventures.

Hidden Motives

Freud proposed that much of our mental life is beyond conscious awareness, that our motives are driven by subconscious desires. Consistently with this, modern social psychology has demonstrated a raft of astonishing ways in which we're influenced by factors that we're unaware of. For example, a study by Aaron Kay and colleagues showed that participants who were sat at a table with a briefcase on it played a financial game more selfishly and competitively than did participants sat at the same table with a backpack on it. Yet afterwards, when asked to explain their playing style, none of the participants mentioned any aspect of the physical environment.

Repression

Freud said that as part of our defence mechanisms, our mind actively represses unpleasant memories. Modern-day researchers have shown that intentional forgetting is indeed possible and does affect the likelihood of memories being recalled in the future. Michael Anderson and colleagues presented participants with unrelated word pairs (for example, ordeal/roach). Later they were presented with the first word from each pair, and asked either to recall its partner or not to think about its partner. Not only was the latter condition associated with a unique pattern of brain activity, repressed words were also harder to recall when tested later on.

6 Personality

THE PROBLEM:

Susan and James are flat-mates looking to rent out their spare room. Unfortunately, they've watched too many horror movies and it's made them fearful of strangers. They want to use psychology to help them make sure that their new lodger isn't an oddball. The pair decide to devise a personality test. But how can they make sure that applicants for their room don't fake their way through the test?

THE METHOD:

We saw earlier in the chapter that most psychologists now believe that personality is made up of five main factors: extraversion, neuroticism, conscientiousness, openness to experience, and agreeableness. Susan and James agree that the most important traits they'd like to see in their new lodger are friendliness and tidiness, which means they need to look out for a high scorer in conscientiousness and agreeableness.

After doing some background reading, the friends discover some basic questionnaire items that can be used to tap into these traits (see p.117 for examples). This process will involve applicants saying whether various descriptive statements apply to their own personality. But it quickly occurs to Susan that if a malevolent oddball were to apply for their room, it will be pretty obvious to him or her that it's a good idea to present their

personality as fitting the profile of a friendly, tidy character, and they'll answer the questionnaire items accordingly.

Indeed, this is a well-known problem in personality testing: people usually want to present themselves in a "socially desirable" light. This is especially the case when people have their personality tested as part of a selection process. One study compared the average personality traits of job applicants against people who weren't applying for a job, and found that the applicants scored higher in all the ways you'd expect if they were trying to make a good impression—the results suggested they were more open-minded, outgoing, conscientious, and emotionally stable.

This implies it's easy to manipulate standard personality tests to present oneself in a favorable light. A friend suggests to Susan and James that they use an ink-blot test or some other "projective" measure of personality that is harder to fake. This would involve the room applicants saying what they saw in each ink blot (see p.115). But the flat-mates agree—although such a test might be hard to fake, it will be jolly hard to interpret too! They want to ask their applicants straight questions about their personality but in a way that isn't easily faked.

THE SOLUTION:

There is a way. Rather than listing a series of personality statements and asking the room applicants to say which ones fit their own personality, Susan and James need to set different desirable statements up against each other. It helps that they specifically want a tidy, friendly lodger. That way they can pitch statements like (a) "I enjoy housework" (a sign of high conscientiousness) up against statements like (b) "I enjoy learning new things" (a sign of high openness to experience).

They can ask applicants which describes you better: (a) or (b)? Applicants are forced to choose one over the other, even though both could be considered desirable.

The psychologists Jacob Hirsh and Jordan Paterson tried out a personality test designed just this way in 2008 and they found it was much more difficult to fake. A faked standard test no longer correlated with real-life outcomes such as school exam performance (as honestly answered tests do). However, the new-fangled test still predicted such outcomes even when participants attempted to manipulate it. Susan and James might find the lodger of their dreams after all   but hang on, how well do they really know each other? Susan's just had a thought: why is James so obsessed with horror films?

7

Stress and Anxiety

Adrenaline-fuelled fear and panic can save our
lives when we experience them at the right times.
For some people, however, these processes are
triggered inappropriately, as part of irrational
phobias or panic disorder. This chapter covers
these conditions. Even when a stress-response is
appropriate, a life-threatening traumatic event can
leave a person with terrible psychological scars.
We'll also look at this phenomenon, known as
post-traumatic stress disorder.

HANDLING CHANGE

Many of the most natural human experiences involve change. In fact change is indivisible from the passage of time. So why can it be so difficult to handle? Speaking in general terms, one of the biggest causes of stress and anxiety is having to adapt to change.

Researchers know that routine experiences get encoded in our brains in specific ways. It has even been shown that things as simple as taking a different route to work, trying to write with the opposite hand to usual, or just being in a room after rearranging the furniture give the brain a healthy, stimulating jolt.

The reality seems to be that we become programmed to our routines, creating an attachment even to things that would otherwise seem quite innocuous. At times, we may have been sad to see the old gas station on the corner torn down, even if we had never been there ourselves, even perhaps if we had considered it an eyesore. We develop attachments to the things we are used to seeing, to doing, and to knowing.

Even when change is "for the better," there tends to be a reaction of anxiety toward it. Almost by definition change

---

HOW DO YOU FEEL ABOUT CHANGE

Which of the following describes you the best?

(a) I tend to get bored in places after doing the same things for too long. I enjoy starting new jobs or new career paths. I am continually seeking new thrills and trying new things, new foods, and new hobbies. I thrive on new experiences and am always making new friends. I love living in different cultures and consider myself a "travel junkie."

(b) I have lived in the same place for a long time and cherish my deep roots and sense of community. I like to know what to expect, and I am more comfortable with routine and stability. I tend to keep the same job for long periods of time, and the friends I see most often are the friends I have had for a long time.

ANSWERS

People who fall in the first category are those who "enjoy change," and may feel stifled if they do not experience it; however, this can still be viewed as staying within their comfort zone and, for them, to change things often can in itself still become a routine.

necessarily means the unknown. Especially as we age, the unknown seems to inspire fear or discomfort to a greater extent.

Adapting to Change

The tendency to seek peace externally instead of internally can also contribute to making change more difficult to adapt to. Often, if we are unhappy, we may look to our lives to see "what needs to be fixed" or "what is to blame." We may make an external change without examining our internal lives to see what we ourselves may have been contributing to the situation in which we were not finding satisfaction. If this is the case, then we can easily find the same complaints or habits emerging in the brand new environment, creating further disappointment and distress.

Several other mechanisms in our thought process can further contribute to making change difficult to adapt to. These include the fact that our thoughts filter our experiences, to such a degree that our perceptions slant toward what can be a distorted reality.

The human process does not work in such a way that we are able to evaluate a single characteristic of an experience individually; instead we unwittingly link a number of characteristics. In some cases we assign related characteristics to what we think we know to be true, causing the perception of the experience to be distorted. It is in this way that the differences between experiences that fall into different categories can be exaggerated, while the differences between experiences that fall into the same category are minimized.

All in all, what is in actuality a minor degree of difference can be perceived as a "world of difference." The implication of this is that it becomes much more difficult to adapt to change, because what is truly only a little different is seen as a huge change.

LOCUS OF CONTROL

FIND YOUR OWN LOCUS OF CONTROL

Mark the box of each statement that you think relates to you.

1. I believe that things happen the way they are meant to. ▢

2. Sometimes, no matter how hard I try, there are factors that I cannot overcome that prevent me from being happy. ▢

3. It's not what you know, it's who you know. ▢

4. Some people are just born winners, and others are born under a bad sign. ▢

5. I often feel like I am just not getting ahead or being recognized, even though I work as hard as I can. ▢

6. When I am not happy or feel stuck I have the power to change things. ▢

7. I work hard for my accomplishments, and I tend to get what I want. ▢

8. When something doesn't go the way I thought it would, I will keep trying different routes until I find something that meets my satisfaction. ▢

9. People who struggle are often weak or lazy. ▢

10. I am able to relate with people and people generally understand me. ▢

SCORE YOURSELF

For each box checked in questions 1 through 5, give yourself one point. For every box checked for questions 6 through 10, subtract a point.

A score nearer to 1—5 reflects that you have a high internal locus of control. People with an internal locus of control take responsibility for their actions and believe they are in charge, making things happen in their lives. People who attribute success to their internal drive are more likely to be motivated, disciplined, and persistent, and have a greater tendency toward planning and setting specific objectives. People with a high locus of control are less prone to depression and anxiety.

Scores closer to + 5 reflect an external locus of control. You tend to feel that life is a large force in and of itself, and you are a piece of the puzzle. People with external loci of control tend to feel at the mercy of outside influences, and may not believe they have the power within themselves to effect or actualize change. These people are more prone to experiencing self-doubt and low self-esteem, anxiety at the uncertainty of meeting expectations, feelings of learned helplessness (see page 81), and other depressive cognitions. However, these people come to terms more easily with unavoidable situations such as terminal illness and natural disasters.

Dating a Control Freak

The "locus of control"—a concept introduced in 1954 by Julian Rotter—tends to be one of the most complicated but important facets of maintaining a healthy relationship. The person with an internal locus of control is, by nature, used to taking charge—they are likely to be capable, directed, and strong willed. On the other hand, a person with an external locus of control is often more flexible, laid-back, and may tend to "go with the flow."

Not surprisingly, these personality types are often attracted to the opposite qualities in one another. The person with an external locus of control may help the one with the internal locus to relax and to "let go," while themselves appreciating the powerful "get things done" attitude of the other. However, this dynamic can easily fall out of balance.

The "external controlist," flexible as they are to the ways of the world, may easily adapt into the ways of the other—and in doing so may unwittingly set a dangerous precedent. While the specific way in which the "internal controlist" likes to do things may also be one avenue of the flexible person's personality, it would likely be only one of many ways in which they might act. The internal person may easily put forth an "only my way" attitude, for that way may be all that they know. In doing this they may not recognize or appreciate that there are other alternative, equally viable ways, or they may simply not be comfortable "following." Because of this they can quite easily steamroller over the more flexible, and often less self-assured party, frequently without realizing the problems they are causing.

THE FAILURE TO MAINTAIN INDIVIDUALISM

Is your partner often angry if you don't clean the bathroom, but when you do so, it's not done "right?" Your other half wants you to do it, but wants you to do it how they would do it…

Take another example, in which a music-loving couple choose concert tickets for the weekend. He loves the opera, but she loves classic rock. Well actually, it's a long time since they've seen a rock band, and she doesn't get around to listening that much at home either, what with the opera being on the stereo all the time. It's not that much of a problem, after all she likes to listen to opera as well; and actually maybe it's not the case that she loves classic rock, so much as she used to love it—or is it?

Of course, change is inevitable, but why do we sometimes let go of our individuality so easily? Actively giving ourselves the space needed to recognize our needs as individuals, examining and challenging unwritten expectations of a relationship that may be unequal, and simply establishing the guidelines to "let you be you, and I'll be me" are some of the most essential tools to keeping a relationship happy. After all, there was a time when you didn't even know each other.

ANXIETY

An experienced rock climber was undertaking a difficult climb when he felt the rocks that he was clinging to suddenly give way. He fell backward toward the ground, with a big chunk of rock falling closely after him.

Sure to be crushed under its weight, he hit the ground, and the rock fell atop him. Incredibly, with a wave of almost supernatural strength, the man was able to "catch" and repel the rock away from him. The man was hurt, but he survived.

Fight or Flight

Our "fight or flight" mechanism is driven by the neuro-chemical hormone adrenaline. When something in our environment is strong enough to trigger the response, it results in a range of psycho-physiological responses to the impending danger. The responses include increased pupil size, so that more information can enter the eye, increased heart rate, so that oxygen can be pumped to the muscles and brain, and greater conversion of glycogen to glucose, so that rapidly contracting muscles and essential organs are supplied with increased energy.

The natural essence of anxiety enables us to remove ourselves from or prepare to combat potentially dangerous situations. While we rarely interpret stress or anxiety as healthy or welcome, the reality is that both are both very natural and often useful guides for decision-making processes.

As a society we have a tendency to qualify emotions and experiences as "good" or "bad," and to rapidly seek to get out of any emotional state that we do not regard as pleasurable. When we don't feel

"well," we continually focus on how to "feel better," and this often means a struggle to fight or drown out our feelings. In reality there are no "bad" emotions. Anxiety, and other emotions that are unpleasant to feel, such as anger or pain, are all natural parts of the human experience. They are all important, and equally valid. It is what we choose to do with these emotions, however, rather than the emotions themselves, that can clearly be good or bad.

Dealing With Stress

Continued stress and anxiety are not feelings to be fought, and may be red flags that something is drastically awry in one's situation. They may be indicators that we need to take a mental inventory, looking critically at our lifestyle, and ask ourselves some difficult questions. They can call us to turn our attention inward.

Today's society has become comfortable with our increased experience of both stress and anxiety, often considering it to be a normal by-product of a successful or productive lifestyle. Certain stress-producing situations may be out of our control, though the number of situations for which that is actually true is fewer than we tend to perceive (see Learned Helplessness on page 81). Our health and well-being are regularly placed as our lowest priority in relation to our desired

achievements, and we often engage in conflict (feeling that we have no other options), or unhealthily internalize issues that would better remain external. Ironically, the times when we are involved in stressful situations seem to be the times when we are less likely to follow the path to seek out our enjoyments or relaxation activities—feeling guilty for "wasting" time away from the focus of our stress, or even for enjoying ourselves in stressful times. If this is the case then we are having the exact opposite behavioral reaction to what is truly needed.

While the experiences of anxiety and stress are natural and inherently useful, they are obviously quite unhealthy when allowed to continue for extended amounts of time. When we receive the benefit of an instantaneous extra jolt of power, overall enhanced abilities, or an extended focus from rising to the occasion in times of stress, it is necessarily on a short-term basis. However, people who dwell on worst-case scenarios, who exaggerate perceived risks, or who project doubt and undue worry are artificially employing anxiety. In doing so, they are continually keeping their fight or flight response in an activated mode. This has the effect of calling to the brain for help, keeping it in a state of continual arousal when no help is truly needed. What ensues is sickness.

ADDICTIVE ANXIETY

The longer we stay in the state of heightened arousal—whether basic irritation or full-on anxiety—the more it may seem to compound itself, and the more difficult it may be for the chemistry of mind and body to return to normal.

There are people who simply seem born into a state of excessive worry. While most of us worry about things from time to time, people who suffer from Generalized Anxiety Disorder (GAD) find themselves in a state of extreme worry nearly all the time, even when their fears are obviously unrealistic. To these people worrying feels like an unavoidable state of mind, and sufferers of GAD are generally unable to "take their mind off it" when they face a problem. GAD therefore can easily interfere with a person's day-to-day life. GAD sufferers often have difficulty enjoying their lives; they may easily find themselves continually distracted by their worries, and have difficulty working, sleeping, and socializing. Not surprisingly, GAD sufferers experience related physical symptoms that include excessive exhaustion or being "highly strung," muscle tension, and related troubles with cardiovascular and immune-system diseases, and gastrointestinal complications.

PANICS AND PHOBIAS

In February 2003, in a town outside of Providence, Rhode Island, what began as a night of music and fun quickly turned dark. Concert-goers filled a club to listen to an old band and see a wild show, filled with pyrotechnics. However, the pyrotechnics went awry, and within three minutes a good time and a great show turned into a conflagration.

THE GOD OF PANIC

The word "panic" itself has an interesting history that sums up the all-embracing terror to which its sufferers can succumb. It stems from the name of the ancient Greek god Pan, the god of shepherds.

Alongside his other associations, among which are erotic love and music, Pan possessed the ability to inspire extreme, irrational fear, particularly in those in isolated places. In fact, the ancient Greeks believed that Pan had put his powers to good use in a battle between the giant titans and the gods. When the former launched an assault on Mount Olympus, Pan blew his conch, inspiring terror in the assailants and causing them to flee in terror, a trick that he reputedly repeated to the Athenians' advantage in their victory at the Battle of Marathon over the invading Persians. Henceforth such irrational terrors have been called *panic*, for the god who instilled such dread in his enemies' hearts.

There were no sprinklers in the venue, which soon filled with black smoke. Panic quickly set in. The crowd rushed to the front entrance. As in many great tragedies, there were stories of heroics and of altruism, of people risking their lives to save the lives of others. However, there also were signs of trampling, especially at the door. Of the 96 people who died that night, most died at the front door, where people had blindly followed one another in sheer terror to the place where they had entered. The club had four other functioning entrances.

Understanding Panic

Panic is an emotional state of blinding fear. It is one that overcomes an individual, replacing all rational and logical thought and often leading people to take actions that they would never otherwise contemplate, even actions that are harmful to their own well-being and would seem to play into the hands of the very fear that has caused them to panic.

What Causes Panic?

Stressful life events can be catalysts that trigger panic disorders, where an individual may suffer one or even repeated panic attacks. In the course of a panic attack the "fight or flight" reaction is triggered, but often with no direct stimulus. In an attack, an individual experiences complete and all-consuming anxiety, the physical symptoms of which closely resemble a heart attack. Such symptoms may include a rapid heart rate, chest pains, chills and trembling, tightness in the throat, a tingling of the extremities, dizziness, shortness of breath, nausea, and feelings of utter doom or dread. A panic episode often begins abruptly, without warning, and peaks in about 10 minutes; however, it can last anywhere from a few minutes to a half-hour or even longer.

Panic Attacks

There are three types of panic attacks: spontaneous, specific, and situational. In the case of spontaneous attacks, there is no direct stimulus. General stress or specific loss is thought to lessen a person's overall threshold, and in this state their underlying physiology becomes predisposed for the switch to flip, and an attack to be triggered. In specific and situational attacks, there is a given stimulus that triggers the attack. The attacks associated with exposure to personal phobias are an example of a specific panic attack, which are likely to develop in places or situations where previous panic attacks have occurred. Likewise, a situational attack will occur under particular circumstances; however, the difference between specific and situational attacks is that while particular catalysts may trigger a situational attack, they are not the object of the panic itself.

As with anxiety, healthy fear is a natural emotion likely designed to protect and direct the self in threatening situations. Babies appear to be naturally afraid of certain potentially threatening stimuli, such as snakes and heights, for example, while they learn over time to be afraid of man-made objects such as guns. It is likely that the development of phobias is a natural response to fear that has gone awry.

A similar model to the disturbances found in panic attacks may be the cause of phobias—extreme fear in specific situations in which there is no real danger, or where the sense of fear is significantly out of proportion to the risk.

There are two theories on the nature of phobias: The non-associative model holds that vulnerability to phobias is largely innate, and does not arise directly from environmental experience. However, the traditional etiologic theories hold that phobias are a result of transmission from others, or social conditioning. Interestingly, some studies have found that certain phobias may be hereditary, though social phobias (in other words, pervasive anxiety at being in social situations) and other specific phobias may differ in this regard.

Overcoming Anxiety

Techniques for overcoming phobias and panic attacks may employ education, psychotherapy, and medication. Exposure to the particular stimulus is generally an important part of treatment. Two examples are "systematic desensitization," a treatment developed by Joseph Wolpe, in which the subject is gradually exposed to the fear, albeit largely in imagined and simulated situations; and "flooding," developed by Thomas Stampfl, where the subject is exposed to the feared stimuli.

POST-TRAUMATIC STRESS DISORDER

Imagine your worst nightmare. Imagine it coming true. Now imagine not being able to stop imagining it. This is what happens to victims of post-traumatic stress disorder (see also pages 40–41), in which they suffer from recurrent, intrusive perceptual and sensory distortions, and the experience is as though the trauma itself were recurring. Symptoms of this debilitating disorder include hallucinations, flashbacks, and vividly accurate dreams.

A Brief History of Trauma

Initially known as "shell shock," the modern-day condition known as post-traumatic stress disorder (PTSD) was first diagnosed among survivors of combat. PTSD is a condition that can result when an individual is involved with a potentially life-threatening event or events, or where grave bodily or emotional harm was potentially suffered by the self or others. Examples of such traumatic experiences include exposure to severe violence, crime, or warfare, natural disasters, sexual abuse, serious accidents, and witnessing trauma to others.

What is PTSD?

The condition of PTSD fundamentally may be disorder of affect-arousal regulation. In other words, once the arousal system becomes flooded, as is the case in a traumatic situation, a switch becomes stuck and can no longer return to "normal," even after the stimulus is removed. This switch, and the patient, remain in constant reactive mode.

It is possible that PTSD victims re-experience their traumas again and again as the stimuli they experienced overloaded the abilities of their cognitive processes, and the brain was unable to consolidate or regulate the related memories and emotions. It is thought that this continual re-experience may be the result of attempts by an oversaturated system to process the still-undigested information.

The shockingly accurate dreams, in which a trauma is played out exactly as it happened, seem to further support the idea of undigested or unprocessed information. The normal encoding that is evident in dream states, the non-linear and non-precise dream storylines that we are all accustomed to—and where we understand that memories are processed and consolidated—is strikingly absent in the dreams of trauma sufferers.

Why Does This Happen to Some Victims, but Not to All?

Two people may experience the same trauma, but be affected by it in drastically different ways. One may simply be "shaken up" but not develop the full-blown symptoms of PTSD, while the other is traumatized and suffers the condition at its worst. Why is this? Research shows associations between PTSD and poorer neurocognitive function, especially involving attention and memory. These deficits are thought to be the consequence of abnormalties in the norepinephrine (a hormone and neurotransmitter) system or of decreased volume in the hippocampus region of the brain, which is associated with PTSD. The question is, do these abnormalities cause a greater vulnerability and likelihood of PTSD occurring in the case of trauma, or does the trauma itself cause these abnormalities? Are individuals with greater memory abilities more successful at suppressing the unwanted intrusive thoughts of PTSD? This has been a very difficult question to answer, as by its very nature trauma itself is unpredictable. Researchers can hardly take a research volunteer, and expose them to trauma to obtain before-and-after measurements.

An Eternal Struggle

Other complications keep PTSD sufferers trapped in their continual struggles as well. Everyday experiences may be perceived as part of the triggering trauma, and an intense, irrational tendency to avoid anything that is remotely related to the trauma may ensue. For example, a backfiring car may be experienced as a gun being fired, or a woman who has been attacked returning to her car after shopping may be unable to go anywhere alone.

Sufferers may have an exaggerated "startle" response. They are likely to experience a pervasive disconnectedness especially from their sense of self, and also suffer from a restricted range of affect or emotion, struggling to find the feelings, interest, or inclination to care much about anything. They may suddenly find it hard to imagine any sense of their future. They may withdraw, and practice avoidance of anything that might trigger their response. Traumatized individuals are constantly oscillating between re-experiencing the trauma and trying to avoid it.

Herbert Benson

For much of medical history, alternative concepts have been scoffed at by traditional, conservative medicine. Practices such as acupuncture, meditation, or yoga were thought of as "far out" practices of hippies or weirdos; any benefit was assumed to be achieved purely in the mind. Today, many of these practices are well respected, and given credence as physical healing powers.

Herbert Benson is an American cardiologist who is largely credited with integrating the "mind–body" approach of alternative medicine to the mainstream, and giving credence to the healing power that the mind can have over the body. While pursuing his cardiology research at Harvard, Dr. Benson was approached by adherents of the Maharishi Mahesh Yogi of Transcendental Meditation fame. The "TM'ers" believed that they could control their blood pressure through their meditative thoughts alone. At the time in medicine, the cardiovascular system was understood as being completely autonomic (functioning automatically on its own). However, Dr. Benson was persuaded to explore the effects of meditative practice in a laboratory setting amidst the conservative Harvard medical community.

The studies of Dr. Benson and the "TM'ers" showed that they were indeed able to lower patients' blood pressure voluntarily. The process they found that achieved this result, was termed the "relaxation response."

Eliciting the relaxation response, in essence, requires two simple steps: In the words of the Benson–Henry Institute for Mind Body Medicine:

1. the repetition of a word, sound, phrase, prayer, or muscular activity.
2. passive disregard of everyday thoughts that inevitably come to mind and the return to your repetition.

The simple fact that the meditative process was shown to evoke the healing process opened the doors for greater awareness of how our thoughts can impact on our physical well-being. Although Dr. Benson began working with people who suffered with high blood pressure, helping them to lower their own blood pressures, he also found far greater benefits including general increases their levels of health and well-being could be acheived through the relaxation technique.

Dr. Benson speaks of the mind being able to "disconnect" from everyday thoughts and worries, calming people's bodies and minds more quickly and to a degree otherwise unachievable. Once the mind reaches a state of deep relaxation, the body is able to relax and repair some of its most important mechanisms, and increase overall immunity.

ACHIEVING THE RELAXATION RESPONSE

If you want to try the relaxation response, follow these steps adapted from the Benson–Henry Institute for Mind–Body Medicine:

1. Sit quietly in a comfortable position.
2. Close your eyes.
3. Relax all your muscles, beginning with your feet and progressing up to your face.
4. Breathe through your nose. Become aware of your breathing. As you breathe out, say the word, "one"— or any soothing, mellifluous sound, preferably with no particular meaning or association, to avoid stimulation of unnecessary thoughts—silently to yourself. For example, breathe in... out, "one"; in... out, "one;" and so on. Breathe easily and naturally.
5. Continue for 10 to 20 minutes. You may open your eyes to check the time, but do not use an alarm. When you finish, sit quietly for a few minutes, first with your eyes closed and later with your eyes opened. Do not stand for a few minutes.
6. Do not worry about whether you achieve a deep level of relaxation. Maintain a passive attitude and permit relaxation to occur at its own pace. When distracting thoughts occur, try to ignore them by not dwelling upon them and return to repeating "one."

With practice, the response should come with little effort. Practice the technique once or twice a day, but not within two hours after a meal, since the digestive processes seem to interfere.

He also stresses the importance of the "Faith Factor," and has claimed that a spiritual belief system increases the benefits and transports the mind–body even more dramatically, quieting worries and fears significantly better than the relaxation response alone. He pushes no one belief system over another, but preaches the importance and necessity of tuning in to one's feelings. He encourages people to trust their instincts more often and more actively. Benson encourages people to commit to their own processes of finding out what is important to them, of tapping into their insides, whether through "soul-searching," "mulling it over," "listening to one's heart," "going inside of one's self," "praying," or "sleeping on it." Some people act on instincts or common sense; others find a truth or intuition emerges slowly. But most people know when something "feels right." Most people have a kind of internal radar that occasionally calls out to them.

According to Benson, trusting the power of this process is paramount in "letting go" of worries and stressors, and embracing thorough relaxation. The challenge to the patient is one of self care, making the relaxation practices daily habits. Such relaxation processes are also quite useful in treating stress and anxiety disorders.

CHILLING FOR ALL THE RIGHT REASONS

The effects of emotional unease on our physical health are widespread and clear as day. Continuous emotional unrest, regardless of how much we may focus on it, affects our mental, physical, and spiritual health negatively. Stress and anxiety can increase blood pressure, interfere with digestive processes, cause muscular tension and resulting complications, and contribute to heart disease and other medical problems.

THE PERFECT PARENT

You are a parent. Your child has many interests and hobbies: art, sports, theater, music, being with friends, being outside in the natural world, traveling to different places and playing games, and so on. Your child loves going to museums, taking the dog to the park, and has a creative imagination. There are countless other things you know your child will enjoy and be very talented at, but hasn't been exposed to yet.

Option A

Wanting to help develop your child's talents and broaden their horizons, you actively seek out activities and adventures you know your child will love. You take an active role in developing interests and skills, and are involved and encouraging.

Option B

While you know there are many things your child enjoys doing, you don't have the time for them. You don't know where to go to find activities and they are often too expensive or far away. Often you are too tired from taking care of the child's basic needs to put the energy into figuring out what to do. Scheduling play dates easily gets put low on the list because of the hassles that can accompany it. Your intentions are good, but sometimes that is all they are—intentions.

As a good parent, you most likely strive to fall in the category of Option A. There may be some unfortunate truths to the reality in Option B, but Option A obviously is an ideal state for a parent to exist in. Now reread the situation and the scenarios. What if we are no longer talking about your child, but we are talking about you? How do your answers change? And how much more likely are you to fall into Option B? We often treat ourselves in ways in which we would not dream of treating others or in ways in which we would never treat a child. We may be emotionally abusive to ourselves, too busy for ourselves, easily placing self-care and simple enjoyment low priority. Stress and anxiety easily make us prone to self-neglect, behaviorally and otherwise. The reality is that stress and anxiety are indicators that we need to do the very opposite.

Anxiety can be the beginning of a dangerous downward spiral if ignored, and often the symptoms are ignored or accepted as a normal part of one's reality. Symptoms of stress or anxiety such as irritability, disrupted sleep, muscle tension, restlessness, inability to concentrate, nausea, regular head- or stomachaches, and ulcers, are often not taken seriously. The reality is that they are often red flags through which our body communicates to us that something in our lives, or our internal processing of our external environment is not right and needs changing.

LEARNING TO RELAX

If these symptoms of stress and anxiety occur frequently and interfere with your physical and emotional well-being, then it may be time to learn a healthier way to cope with anxiety. Relaxation techniques can especially help patients with cardiac disease, hypertension, anger, angina, arrhythmia, diabetes, pain, high cholesterol, sleep problems, stress-related disorders, and even those who are preparing for or recovering from surgery. Relaxation is shown to promote long-term health and improve the quality of life in patients dealing with serious health problems.

Therapeutic relaxation techniques help teach the mind to slow down and focus on breathing in order to reconnect with the body. The purpose is to bring our bodies back to a state of equilibrium, or balance, following disruptions that put stress on all the systems the body regulates. This is done by learning to reach a state of "thoughtless awareness" from intrusive thoughts and maintaining focus on the body sensations that produce muscular and mental release.

There are many types of relaxation techniques and it is important to find the one(s) that work best for you. Here are just a few examples:

Progressive Muscle Relaxation
Visualization
Deep Abdominal Breathing
Guided Imagery
Art Therapy
Meditation
Yoga
Aromatherapy
Music Therapy
Prayer

There are also a number of tests to take online to see how many symptoms of stress and anxiety apply to you. Typing "anxiety risk assessment" into a search engine will provide you with plenty of examples.

7 Stress and Anxiety

THE PROBLEM:

It's been a nightmare day. You had a furious row with your boss this morning which ended with her threatening to hit you with a formal misconduct charge. Later, as you were driving home alone through sheets of rain, you pranged a parked car, denting both vehicles. At last, you're indoors. Sat at the dining table, stressed out, head in hands, you glance up and see a notepad and pen. How can these items possibly help you to feel better?

THE METHOD:

After you spy the pad of paper, various options enter your mind. You could make paper aeroplanes. That might entertain you for a minute or two, but it's hardly likely to ease the knots of anxiety twisting in your stomach. What about drawing a picture of your boss and throwing darts at it? Could be cathartic, but you'll probably damage the wall, and you don't have any darts anyway. No, what I suggest you try is expressive writing.

There are different approaches you could take. You could try writing about the day's incidents and how they made you feel. Alternatively, maybe your stress levels are more deep-rooted. Are there any issues from your past that still trouble you? You could write about these issues or events and how they make you think and feel. Or, finally, what about writing a poem or story that has nothing directly to do with the stress of today or the past? What about letting your creative side have free reign and seeing what you come up with?

THE SOLUTION:

The therapeutic benefits of expressive writing are well-documented. When a group of participants are asked to make time over several days to write about troubling or emotional episodes from their past, studies have shown the benefits they enjoy compared with control participants who merely write about something neutral. The expressive writers typically suffer a dip in mood at first, but over time, after performing several writing exercises, they come to enjoy better mental and physical health than the control participants.

It's not entirely clear why expressive writing has these benefits but a popular theory is that it allows people to fit their experiences into a narrative. By editing

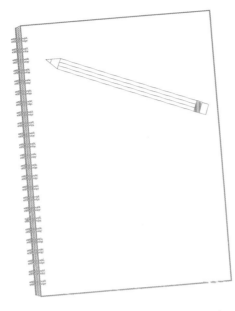

and re-working what they've written, people can make sense of what happened to them. The practice can also generate feelings of control, which as we heard on p.134, can be vital for reducing stress.

Writing fictional stories and poems can also be therapeutic, in large part because it's a lot of fun. Similar to writing more directly about traumatic experiences, writing stories or poems can also offer a way to work through delicate issues but this time via the lives and events of a fictional world. Longer term, when people join creative writing workshops, this can also offer an opportunity for making new friends and give people a feeling of belonging.

Alternatively, creative writing can be used in conjunction with conventional therapy. Many people find it easier to express their problems to a therapist indirectly through the medium of creative writing. A trained therapist will reflect on the stories with a client. They may also read stories or poems written by others to the client, inviting the client to respond to the issues and relationships in those stories.

If lengthy expressive writing doesn't sound like your thing, there's some other research that could be useful. A study published in 2010 found that simply writing down a regretted decision and sealing it in an envelope helped generate a feeling of psychological closure. Students who did this enjoyed better mood than other students who merely wrote the problem down but didn't put it in an envelope. "We have shown that the metaphorical act of enclosing and sealing influences the memory, in the sense that the recollection of the emotional details of an event becomes weaker," said the researchers who were based at the National University of Singapore.

Chapter

8

Sleep

Add up all the time you spend snoozing in bed and
it comes to years and years. You'd think we'd all be
experts and yet many people's lives are blighted by
sleep problems including insomnia, sleep walking
and nightmares. This chapter explores what
happens if we don't get the sleep we need, as well
providing tips for how to get a good night's kip.

SLEEP PARASOMNIAS

Stan Taylor was principal of one of the largest high schools in a medium-sized city. He was well known and well liked, always knowing students' names and having a smile or a kind word for those he passed. He was a respected figure in the local community, as were his parents before him. He was involved in the city council, and in charity work, was an avid runner, and was happily married for 30 years, having raised three successful children.

Faces drained white the morning Mrs. Taylor walked into her office with bruises and scratches all up and down her arms and face. "What on earth happened?" her colleagues cried out, "Who did this to you?" Mrs. Taylor looked down and hesitated, not knowing how to respond. Slowly, she looked up, tears filling her eyes. "Stan did," she whispered. Gasps of disbelief filled the otherwise silent room. "He..." she stammered, "He was... asleep."

Stan Taylor is an example of the most commonly studied parasomnia, REM Sleep Behavior Disorder (RBD) where the person is in REM sleep and acts out violent dreams through body movements and sounds.

What's Happening?

In essence, this is a state of partial arousal. The body displays behaviors associated with being awake and asleep, simultaneously. During these phenomena called parasomnias, a person will perform what are often complex physical and verbal behaviors, including ones that are dangerous—all while in the mind–body state that we define as sleep.

BEHAVIORS ACTED OUT IN RDB CAN INCLUDE:

Yelling
Cursing
Punching
Strangling
Driving
Firing guns
and more...

There tends to be a correlation between the acted-out behavior and subject content reported in a dream.

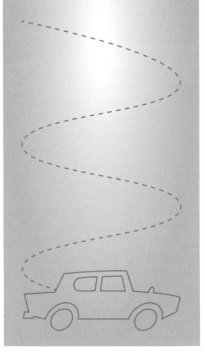

The Case of Mr. Dorff

One of the strangest and most famous examples of sleep parasomnia is the case of Mr. Dorff. A patient of Dr. Carlos H. Schenck, Mr. Dorff was a retired grocer who sought treatment at the Mayo Clinic in the U.S. for what he called his "violent moving nightmares." Indeed his nightmares were literally both violent and moving, and in one dream Mr. Dorff ran smack into his bedroom dresser believing that he was a quarterback on the verge of making a touchdown.

Causes of Parasomnias

Why are these physiological systems aroused at inappropriate times? In 1953, Nathaniel Kleitman and his assistant Eugene Aserinsky found that measurements from an electroencephalogram (a device for measuring electrical activity in the brain),

during the "rapid eye movement," or REM, stage of sleep in which the majority of dreaming occurs gave readings similiar to the pattern of electrical activity that is seen during wakefulness.

Although not all parasomnia behavior takes place in REM sleep, scientists have found that during REM the brain sends the same signals to muscles to perform the movements that would be accurate if the person were awake. For most people, during REM sleep another brain circuit simultaneously sends inhibitory chemical signals to the muscles, paralyzing them so as not to perform the instructions. This inhibition applies to all muscles in the body except the diaphragm, one small muscle in the ear, and the muscles that move the eyes. Neurons in certain areas of the mid-brain are known to suppress movement and are implicated in some parasomnias. Interestingly, it is the same region affected in sufferers of Parkinson's disease, and a disproportionate number of parasonmia sufferers develop Parkinson's disease later in life, further supporting the theory that this area of the brain is responsible.

Behind the physical causes lie deeper reasons such as biological dysfunction, stress, and depression—which between them are some of the most common underlying factors. It is also interesting to note that parasomnias tend to be more common in children than adults, and can sometimes run in families.

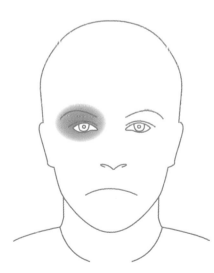

SLEEP DEPRIVATION

We can easily notice the effect of even minimal sleep deprivation. Our thoughts don't seem as sharp, our motor responses seem slow, and our moods are easily affected. In fact there is an undeniable connection between our sleep and our mood, and the link between clinical depression and disrupted sleep is nearly perfect—it is worth noting that disruption of normal sleep is one of the primary criteria for a diagnosis of depression.

It is also worth considering the impact of extreme deprivation on torture victims who are forced to remain awake for extended periods of time, and who report visual and auditory hallucinations as they near the brink of madness. The complications of insomnia and sleep deprivation are multifold, and it is obvious to us all that without proper sleep it's nearly impossible to have a proper mood. But why? Why should fatigue not be able to exist independently from mood disturbance?

The Pattern of Sleep

With both insomnia and excessive sleep, as occurs in depression, it's not simply a matter of more or less time spent in sleep. The whole normal, healthy sleep cycle is torn to pieces.

The pattern of healthy sleep includes four to six separate cycles per night through periods of progressively deeper, more relaxing, slow-wave sleep, which are interspersed with stages of REM sleep that involve high amounts of brain activity and rapid eye movements.

The Purpose of Sleep

One of the functions of sleep is to facilitate the consolidation of memory. REM sleep has been found to be involved with emotional memory. Sleep researchers have found that depressed people enter the REM stage more quickly than normal. They then stay in it longer, and experience more brain activity than normal. Researchers believe that in clinical depression, the loss of slow-wave sleep and

VAN GOGH'S EAR

If Vincent Van Gogh were alive today, it seems he would more than likely receive a diagnosis of bipolar disorder. This disorder can include episodes of mania where the person experiences hallucinations, which is thought to have been the case with Van Gogh. It seems quite possible, that the infamous incident in which he cut off part of his ear may have been an attempt at removing the source of his auditory hallucinations. He did not remove the entire ear, as legend portrays, but instead severed off part of the ear. Interestingly, from our point of view, it is common for those with bipolar disorder to have difficulties sleeping, and the fact that Van Gogh struggled with recurrent insomnia might be a useful indicator in this retrospective diagnosis.

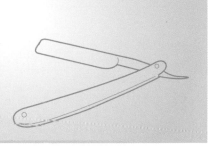

the rush to REM sleep have a detrimental effect on the way memories consolidate and the way that the REM system regulates mood. The increase in REM sleep in the depressed is thought to lead to an over-consolidation of negative memory, causing the sleeper to wake with an extra amount of bad things to think about, because the negative feelings have not been processed and stored away properly.

The disturbances are thought to interfere with the perception of reality around the time of falling sleep, causing patients with insomnia to overestimate the time it takes them to fall asleep and underestimate the amount of time they actually spend sleeping.

Insomnia is the most common sleep disorder, and people who suffer from it have difficulty both falling and staying asleep. It is worth noting that those who suffer from insomnia usually average six full hours of sleep—not a desperately small amount, yet little enough to disrupt the normal sleep cycle, which is where the problems start to arise.

Sleep disturbance results in reduced concentration and decreased reaction time during waking hours, leading to reduced productivity and greater risk of accidents. Amazingly, insomnia affects around a third of adults at some point in their lives, especially during periods of stress. Chronic insomnia is thankfully less common; it may be caused by a number of factors in addition to stress, including imbalances in body chemistry or other medical conditions.

SLEEPWALKING AND SLEEPTALKING

Although frequently a source of mirth, the twin problems of sleepwalking and sleeptalking can have serious consequences, and also provide interesting insights into the sleeping brain.

MULTI-TASKING

Read this paragraph while singing the chorus to *A Hard Day's Night*, or for that matter any other song you like:

"The recent thefts of priceless pieces of art from major museums across the world have left the international art community in a state of anger, shock, and despair. Thieves have broken through top-level security systems in museums and private residences; collective losses total billions of dollars."

As you may have found for yourself, it is nearly impossible to gain the full meaning of the sentences while simultaneously recalling and singing the song. That is because your focus is divided, meaning you cannot fully tune into the two channels at once. Just like in normal sleep, where sleeping inhibits other active processes. However, in parasomnias such as sleepwalking and talking in one's sleep it appears as if the opposite is taking place—in these malfunctions it is almost as if the brain is attempting to tune into two very separate frequencies at the same time.

Somnambulism

Sleepwalking (for which the medical term is somnambulism) most often occurs during deep, non-REM sleep early in the night. If it occurs during REM sleep, it is part of REM behavior disorder and tends to happen closer to morning. The process of sleepwalking involves a sudden arousal from non-REM sleep. When someone sleepwalks, they may sit up and look as though they are awake, while they are actually asleep. They may leave the bed, walk around, or even perform complex activities such as cleaning, moving furniture, going to the bathroom, brushing teeth, getting dressed, or even driving. While a sleepwalking episode can be very brief, lasting just a few seconds or minutes, it can also continue for over a half-hour.

Myth has it that it can be very dangerous to awaken a sleepwalker: This is not true, though the person may be very confused or disoriented upon awakening. It is also a surprisingly common misconception, albeit a slightly foolish one, that sleepwalkers cannot be injured; in reality sleepwalkers often hurt themselves through falling and tripping.

Symptoms of Somnambulism

So how do you tell a sleepwalker apart from someone who has just got up for a zzZzzzzzZZzzzZ

glass of water in the night? Well, the first clue is that they have their eyes open when they otherwise appear asleep—they may have a blank look on their face, or may sit up and appear awake.

They may even leave the bed, walking during sleep or engaging in other detailed activity of any type during sleep. However, sleepwalkers do not remember the sleepwalking episode upon awakening, and will be disoriented if awakened suddenly.

Sleepwalking can occur at any age, but it happens most often in children aged between four and eight, and it appears to run in families.

Somniloquy

Somniloquy, quite literally "sleep talking," does not appear to be detrimental to the sleeptalker's mental or physical well-being. Although classified as a parasomnia, talking during sleep is generally considered of no medical or psychological consequence, and people who talk while asleep have no awareness that they are talking. Often they will wake when their sleeptalking startles another person, who then makes a noise at being woken up, waking the sleeptalker to ask the other "What's wrong?"

Sleeptalking can occur at any point in the sleep cycle, though the lighter the

sleep stage, the more intelligible the speech tends to be. In light sleep people may have entire conversations while asleep; however, in heavy sleep they may be restricted to moans and gibberish. Sleeptalking may occur in any stage of non-REM sleep or REM sleep. It is still unknown whether the talking is closely linked to dreaming, though people intuitively associate sleeptalking with dreaming. While it is possible to talk in REM sleep, it isn't as likely as at other stages due to the muscular inhibition during the REM cycle, which usually imobilizes the jaw and speech mechanisms.

Sleeptalking that is related to RBD or sleep terrors is much more dramatic than that seen otherwise. As a part of RBD, talking may be loud, emotional, and even profane! Talking during sleep terrors tends to involve intense fear, with sufferers screaming and shouting.

What's the Problem?

Somniloquy is not generally considered a serious problem unless other disorders, such as somnambulism and apnea, are involved. However, anxiety disorders, stress, and fevers often make people talk more. The cause of somniloquy is unknown, but around five percent of adults are reported to talk regularly in their sleep. If you're one of those, then the following may help to decrease sleeptalking: avoiding heavy meals before bedtime; getting enough rest—sleep deprivation increases somniloquy; reducing stress levels; and practicing healthy sleep patterns.

NARCOLEPSY

THE TRUTH ABOUT NARCOLEPSY

1. A person suffering from Narcolepsy may typically sleep between 10 to 16 hours per day.

2. Dreaming while awake—including visual and auditory hallucinations—is a symptom of narcolepsy.

A Lack of Boundaries

Narcolepsy is a disorder of boundary disturbances between the states of sleep and wakefulness. As we know, during REM sleep the brain is very active—mimicking the state of wakefulness while the muscles are inhibited. In the normal sleep cycle, the onset of the REM stage occurs between 80 to 100 minutes after the person goes to sleep. A full sleep cycle is 110 minutes, beginning with non-REM sleep, progressing gradually into REM, and then back to non-REM. In narcolepsy, the person enters the REM stage nearly immediately after going to sleep, or sometimes even while still awake. This near-immediate rush into REM sleep from wakefulness can be likened to a continuation of the active brain state of wakefulness, instead of the normal inactive transition through the non-REM stage, with a sudden rather than gradual onset of muscular inhibition. The brain "stays awake," while the body is suddenly put to sleep. Sleep attacks can last anything from a few moments to over an hour.

The transitions from non-REM to REM sleep are controlled by interactions among groups of neurons in the part of the brain stem known as the pons. Scientists believe that narcolepsy results from a malfunctioning or possible degeneration

in these mechanisms that regulate the transitions.

In addition to the characteristic sudden onset of sleep in unusual or active situations, narcolepsy likewise involves other, related complications.

The Condition of Cataplexy

The related condition of cataplexy is a sudden loss of muscle strength that leads to feelings of weakness and a loss of voluntary muscle control. Cataplectic attacks vary in duration and severity. The loss of muscle tone can be slight enough to involve only a slight twinge of weakness in a limited number of muscles, such as mild drooping of the eyelids. However, it can be severe enough to result in a complete loss of tone in all voluntary muscles, leading to a total physical collapse. The person is rendered unable to move, or speak, or keep their eyes open. This, needless to say, is terrifying for the person in question, especially at the first experience. This loss of muscle tone resembles that which normally occurs during REM sleep, and scientists have found that the group of neurons inactive in REM sleep that inhibits muscle movement is likewise inactive in the case of cataplexy.

Other related conditions of narcolepsy involve episodes of paralysis upon wakening or when falling asleep, vivid, dreamlike visual and auditory hallucinations while not asleep, and sudden, rapid jolting from deep sleep into full wakefulness, often with paralysis. All of these symptoms are recognizable from the various phases that we understand occur within the normal phases of sleep. However, all are quite terrifying outside the course of sleep.

Combating Narcolepsy

Narcolepsy has been a mystery until very recently; it is only since the late 1990s that scientists—with those at the Center for Narcolepsy, Stanford School of Medicine at the forefront—have gained an understanding of the causes. In order to combat these, stimulants have been used by doctors as a way to try to prevent the daytime onset of sleep, while certain kinds of antidepressants have been shown to decrease symptoms as well. This finding is an interesting footnote to the discussion earlier on pages 152–53 regarding the relationship between mood and sleep.

LIVING WITH NARCOLEPSY: A THOUGHT EXPERIMENT

Imagine trying to maintain a sense of a normal, safe life while managing the complications of narcolepsy. The minor periods of inappropriate sleep may last only a few moments, during which automatic behavior often takes over, and the action being undertaken appears to continue uninterrupted. But, often narcolepsy is much more severe and more complicated. Imagine the danger involved in everyday tasks such as driving. Or in any public outing, would you feel comfortable carrying a purse or wallet, knowing you may fall asleep while shopping? How would you manage arranging to meet someone? Turning on a stove top and cooking? What about caring for a small child?

The problems faced by those who suffer from narcolepsy underline the fact that the predictability of our consciousness may be something we often take for granted.

LIFE WITHOUT DREAMS

Our dreams, our deepest desires for ourselves, our ideal future—what would life be like without dreams? Have you ever wondered if such questions were mere semantics, or perhaps prompt deeper insights into our neural mechanisms or subconscious?

In the Absence of Dreams

Though it is known that most people do dream every night—given normal functioning brain status—there is a wide variation in people's ability to recall their dreams, which is the reason behind some people believing that they do not dream. Studies on patients who literally do not dream due to brain damage in specific locales, however, have provided interesting information about the nature of dreams themselves.

Damage to an area in the forebrain responsible for spatial recognition and the generation of imagery (the inferior parietal lobe) can be responsible for the brain not entering a dream sequence—hardly a surprising finding given the image-based nature of dreams. However, it is also interesting to note that when damage occurs to an area in the white matter at the bottom of the frontal lobes that drives motivation, dreams are also stopped.

Remembering Your Dreams

It is when we awaken during highly active REM sleep that we have the sudden feeling of "switching gears," where we wake up in what seems to be the middle of a dream, or wake up saying "I was just having a dream about…" For a period of time, one's memory accessing the dream is at its clearest, and details can be recounted at a level that soon fades away.

There is a wide variation among people's abilities to recall dream content, and it is indeed an imperfect science, but for those who have poor dream recall, exercises can be employed to help. (See Improving Your Dream Recall, right.) It is thought that fear of nightmares, or other anxieties or misguided beliefs about dreams and the unconscious, can block dream recall, and these can usually be overcome by learning about the useful nature of dreams and by recognizing that the majority of nightmares may represent opportunities for personal healing through much-needed emotional release.

Reconstructing the Dream

Social psychology has shown that we orient our cognition of the past by how we feel in the present (see page 72). One experiment showed that couples whose marriages ended in failure were subsequently unable to recall a time when the marriage was positive, even though when they were surveyed around the time of the wedding the results indicated that the majority of couples reported being very happy. This construct may also be true for those with low ability to recall their dreams. When memories of one's dream experiences are not readily available, it is hypothesized that one's beliefs about dreams are based on one's current affective state.

IMPROVING YOUR DREAM RECALL

Here are a few tips to help you improve your dream recall:

Keep a dream journal next to your bed. The moment you awake, or at any time that you are struck with memories of a dream, record as much detail as you can recall. Include images, feelings, words utilized. This technique is shown to improve over time, so don't get frustrated if at first you can recall very little. Include notes about your own recent affect (emotional state), things or people that have been on your mind, and the quality of your sleep. Start to look for patterns or recurring themes in your dreams. You may also roll over and jot down notes in the middle of the night if you awake, or keep a tape recorder.

Stay in bed for 15 minutes after you awaken in a relaxed mode—this may help you remember dream details.

Use meditation and relaxation exercises, to help tap into your subconscious mind.

Assert that you will remember your dreams when you are still awake.

Visualize your dreams.

Setting an alarm to wake yourself periodically during the night may keep your brainwave activity at a higher rate. It may be more difficult to access dreams that occurred during the night if we have already finished a sleep cycle, or wakened and returned to deep sleep. Periodic waking may allow you to catch yourself in the act of dreaming and record it quickly. However, while this may help improve your dream recall it is not particularly advisable, as it will impair the quality of your sleep, perhaps resulting in some of the symptoms of sleep deprivation discussed on pages 152–3.

The most important element of trying to remember your dreams is actively cultivating an awareness through consistent practice of the above exercises.

NIGHTMARES

Dreams, and especially "bad" dreams, can help make us aware of the things that we may be most psychologically entrenched in. The dreams themselves may serve to process some of the issues, and can serve as a guide to what we should focus on to remedy our current struggles.

DO YOU RECOGNIZE ANY OF THESE DREAMS?

It is difficult to know just how dreams link to our waking lives, but that hasn't stopped psychologists from trying to find out—one of the most famous books in the field is Freud's *The Interpretation of Dreams*.

Why not see what you can find out from your dreams? Below are some themes and common associations with which they are attributed. This is far from exact, but try to re-experience the feeling of the dream, and be aware of similar feelings in your waking life.

Dream One You tend to have dreams where you are being chased or under attack.

Dream Two You are on stage and don't know your lines, or unprepared for a final exam.

Dream Three You are invisible, or need help and cannot get anyone's attention.

Dream Four You are falling.

Dream Five There is an accident or disaster.

Dream Six You dream of injury to your body.

Dream Seven You are searching for someone or something you cannot find.

Interpretation One Being chased or under attack may indicate part of your personality you have not paid attention to, the existence of repressed feelings, or part of the past that you feel is unresolved.

Interpretation Two Examine aspects of your life or yourself where you are not feeling confident or where you feel embarrassed.

Interpretation Three Do you feel like you are not making an impact in your world, or are you feeling disrespected?

Interpretation Four Are you weighted down by responsibilities? Are you feeling unsupported, or ungrounded?

Interpretation Five Does something feel outside of your abilities of control? Are you overextended?

Interpretation Six Are you feeling guilty or neglectful in some area of your life (other than the body)?

Interpretation Seven Are you feeling dissatisfied?

CONTROL YOUR DREAMS, CONTROL YOUR LIFE

As is the case with the interpretation of dreams, it is difficult to understand the links between your dreaming self and your waking self. However, some people assert that the commitment to listening to what your dreaming self is saying can allow a subtle but powerful control over your waking life. And it can also improve the quality of your dreams.

Using the techniques described in Improving Dream Recall on page 159 try bringing more awareness to your dreaming life with the following steps:

1. Deliberately cultivate a relationship with your dreaming self.
2. Just prior to sleeping, dedicate a given amount of time to the process—you may start with smaller periods of time and increase over time.
3. Cultivate a space that is peaceful; utilize dim lighting, perhaps candles.
4. Select a given issue that has been on your mind. Focus on the issue, rehearsing and repeating the thoughts in your mind.
5. Create images in your mind of things that are associated with the issue. You can gather photos, newspaper clippings, anything concrete that represents the issue. Stare at the objects or close your eyes and focus in your mind's eye.
6. Create a deliberation within yourself. Imagine yourself taking control of the situation. Visualize yourself literally performing actions, talk yourself through conversations. Guide both your real-life experience and the dream process. If you dreamed you were trapped in a sinking box last night, envision yourself bursting out of the box and swimming toward the finish line of a triathlon. Visualize your outcomes, seeing yourself in what you envision things to be like when they have been changed.

7. You may find that deep-breathing exercises or the steps used to elicit the relaxation response (see page 143) can amplify the results of this process.
8. You may also have success by imagining your dreaming self taking control in your dreams, and also by keeping a journal of the desired results.
9. Dedicate yourself to this process. The brain and human experience is an often mysterious and complex realm, but it is one over which we are able to assert our will and our conscious deliberation.
10. Sweet dreams!

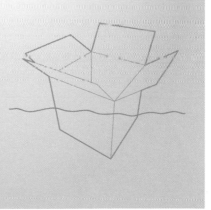

Stanley Coren

Stanley Coren is a psychologist who has done extensive research on sleep habits and the often disastrous results of our sleep-deprived society. He challenges the notion that sleep deprivation is a mere inconvenience—as it is generally dismissed in today's world—and portrays the cumulative sleep debt we develop with continued lack of sleep as a much larger and pervasive detrimental influence on human efficiency and function. His book *Sleep Thieves* provides disturbing and fascinating examples of the harm and potential harm caused by societies' misinformed views and the consequent unhealthy sleep habits.

Coren asserts that individuals require 8 to 10 hours of sleep per 24-hour period, which is what occurs in natural circumstances free from the interference of artificial light sources, such as in the Antarctic season when the sun does not

set. The average seen throughout most modern industrial societies is from 7 to 7.5 hours. Coren also believes we operate from a framework of cumulative sleep debt which gets worse and worse as time continues if our full sleep needs are not met.

Sleeping Baby

Coren notes that a newborn baby will sleep for 16 to 20 hours per day in what is a very active and animated sleep. Newborns are thought to spend 50 percent of their sleeping time dreaming. This fact, he notes, completely puzzled scientists. If dreamwork is meant for the purpose of consolidating memory and working out situations encountered during the day, how could a newborn who is awake so few hours and has so little to process need so much "processing" time… to deconstruct the diaper changes? Coren answers this question by citing results of studies that show that babies in utero at 25 weeks dream nearly all the time. It is held that dreams serve to stimulate parts of the brain in the unstimulating environment of the womb, and are thought to assist in the development of brain tissue. Dreams "exercise" the infant's senses, so upon entering the world the adjustment is much less shocking!

Daylight-saving time creates an unnatural and significant jump, in our sleep cycle, according to Coren. One of his studies shows that the numbers of traffic accidents increase by about 7 percent during the days following the jump and industrial accidents increase by around 6 percent.

DISTURBING TALES FROM THE FILES OF SLEEP DEPRIVATION

In his 1997 book *Sleep Thieves*, Stanley Coren details a number of different case studies in which the effects of sleep deprivation are startlingly profound. Here are just a few short examples.

Sleepless in Surgery

Until recently, medical residents regularly worked 100-hour weeks, frequently entailing continuous shifts of 24 to 36 hours, while other staff also moonlighted or worked comparable continuous shifts. In Denver in 1995, anesthesiologist Joseph Verbrugge Jr. was charged with manslaughter and held responsible for the death of an eight-year-old boy undergoing a routine ear operation. Witness testimony held that Dr.Verbrugge fell asleep several times during the surgery, remaining asleep in one instance for 20 minutes. Since he was asleep, he did not notice the alarming change in vital signs until he awoke, too late.

Keep on Trucking

A truck driver named Joe was one of a series of Coren's interviewees. Joe recounted that his work involved two to three weeks on the road per trip, full cross-country trips, where distances of 900 miles per day were needed. Some of the jobs held bonuses for early arrival, some had penalties for late delivery. Joe tells his worst story, driving across the flat land of Utah, where he started to feel some bumps in the road and couldn't find the white line. Figuring it was just roadworks, he didn't think much about it and kept on trucking.

He eventually stopped, got out of the cab, and peered into the darkness. Seeing nothing, he returned to the cab and fell asleep. He awoke to flashing lights and an officer pounding on the door. His truck had been spotted by a patrol plane from above. Joe's big rig was ten miles off the highway, in the middle of nowhere. He could only guess at having fallen asleep and kept on driving. The flat landscape gave no clue as to the direction back to the highway. It is not uncommon for people to get lost in the desert and never find their way back—he could have driven on with limited fuel, searching for that elusive highway.

Edison's Curse

Society's drastic reduction in sleep habits largely resulted from the invention of the lightbulb. In fact, Edison actively touted the fact that he never slept more than four to five hours a day, and strongly asserted his view that people who slept more hours were lazy.

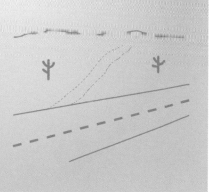

HEALTHY SLEEP

If you are hitting the snooze button in the morning, it means you are not getting enough sleep. Don't laugh. If you are getting enough sleep, you wake up easily and automatically, refreshed. For our sleep-deprived societies it may seem like a fantasy world, but this should be the norm.

HOW TO GET A GOOD NIGHT'S SLEEP

Set a regular schedule: Since our sleep–wake cycle is regulated by our circadian (daily) "clock" in our brain, many people with regular sleep schedules find they often wake up a minute or two before the alarm is set to sound. Keeping the same schedule, ideally including weekends, strengthens the circadian function, helps with sleep onset at night, and improves regularity of sleep cycles, which helps with overall sleep quality.

Set the scene: A relaxing routine before bedtime can help prepare your senses and your body for sleep. Relaxation activities can include those already discussed, along with herbal tea or warm milk, yoga, meditation, soaking in a hot bath. Pursue your pre-bedtime routine in dim lighting, and avoid bright lighting which signals the brain that it should be getting alert as it would in morning, not winding down.

No more pillow talk: Avoid stimulating activities before bedtime, including exciting television shows, intense reading, bill paying, or having emotionally invigorating conversations.

Control yourself: Distractions such as street noise, street lights, or a partner snoring can make it difficult to enter or remain in deep sleep. While it may initially be difficult to get used to earplugs, eye shades, noise machines (that drown out other noise), and other approaches, means taken to control external activation can be beneficial in getting a good night's rest.

Avoid looking at the clock, which tends to cause anxiety through worrying that you won't get a good night's sleep. The anxiety itself then makes it difficult to fall asleep.

Use the bed only for sleeping.

Exercise, but not within three hours of bedtime.

Avoid caffeine or stimulants before sleep. They can affect the sleep pattern even when it's not perceptible to you when awake. Likewise, alcohol should be avoided before bedtime; even though it is thought of as a sedative, it keeps you in the light stages of sleep. Also avoid heavy eating or rich foods before bedtime.

Psychology: Adventures in Perception and Personality

A Short History of Sleep

For much of our history, sleep was considered a single block of time when our brain and body turned off, giving us a rest. However, over the past few decades, we have gained the understanding that the brain is very much active while the "body" sleeps, and know that there are very distinct things that happen in different stages of sleep. We know that certain stages help us feel energized and focused the next day, while other stages consolidate memory, or affect mood regulation. Furthermore, deep sleep triggers release of growth hormone, which fuels growth in children, and helps build muscle mass and repair cells and tissues in children and adults. Another type of hormone, levels of which are increased during sleep, works to fight various infections, which may explain why, when your body is sick, all it wants to do is sleep, and why healthy sleep habits help keep you from getting sick. The hormones released during sleep also affect how the body uses energy, and studies find that the less people sleep, the more likely they are to be overweight or obese, to develop diabetes, and to prefer eating foods that are high in calories and carbohydrates.

So, now you know, deciding to take that extra hour to work, clean, party, or stay up to study for an exam, may just end up costing you more than you think.

Sleep

THE PROBLEM:

Johnny is studying psychology while also putting in countless hours working as a waiter. He's been given his latest work rota and is comparing it against his study schedule. It's a juggling act, but there is scope for flexibility. Johnny realizes he has several sleep-related choices to make: should he avoid working late nights, and if so, should he use that time for nocturnal study? Mondays he has piano practice—should he opt to have it in the afternoon or evening? Finally, there are two available revision sessions for psychology—should he choose Thursday afternoon or Thursday evening?

THE METHOD:

As we heard on page 152, sleep is incredibly important for learning so Johnny is right to make these decisions carefully. Sleeping consolidates factual material and skills that have been learned in the daytime. There's also evidence that a good night's sleep is important for the ability to learn the following day.

Consider a study conducted in 2009 by Ysbrand Van Der Werf and his colleagues. They tested the effects of deliberately waking students with a beep every time they feel into deep, slow-wave sleep. These students had just as much total sleep time as a comparison group of students, but they were denied the all-important periods of deep sleep. The next day, the sleep-disturbed students were less able to commit to memory a series of pictures of houses and landscapes. Even so, for a working student like Johnny, who is so pushed for time, it must be tempting to use the late hours to catch up with his studies.

Regarding when to schedule piano practice and revision sessions, there's relevant research here too. The important detail Johnny should note is that piano playing is a form of "procedural learning" (like riding a bike), whereas the revision sessions will mostly be about learning facts, which involves "declarative memory".

THE SOLUTION:

Johnny should opt to have his piano lesson on Monday evening and his psychology revision session on Thursday afternoon. We know this thanks to a study conducted by Johannes Holz and his co-workers in 2012. They tested girls' performance on a finger-tapping task and a word-learning task. Those girls who learned the tapping task right before bedtime performed better at it when re-tested 24 hours or 7 days later, as compared with girls who learned the finger tapping in the afternoon. By contrast, it was the girls who learned the word-pairs in the afternoon who performed better when tested 24 hours later. In other words, factual material, but not procedural skills, seem to benefit from a period of waking before being consolidated by sleep. What about avoiding late-night restaurant work and using that time for studies? If he can, Johnny should avoid working late nights as a waiter, but burying himself in nocturnal study probably isn't a good idea because it will interfere with his ability to understand his lectures the next day. We saw with the research by Van Der Werf that a good night's sleep is important for learning the next day. Also relevant is a study published in 2012 by psychologists in Los Angeles, which looked specifically at the study habits of hundreds of students. Cari Gillen-O'Neel and her colleagues found that late-night study at the expense of sleep back-fires by interfering with academic performance the next day. If Johnny wants to devote more time to study, he should look for a daytime activity to sacrifice, rather than losing his all-important sleep.

INDEX OF PSYCHOLOGISTS

Kandel, Eric
Major work:
The neurobiology of memory
(p26, 32–3)

Kihlstrom, John
Major work:
Disociative disorders (p123)

Kleitman, Nathaniel
Major work:
Causes of parasomnias (p151)

Lazarus, Richard
Major work:
Theories of emotion (p89)

Libet, Benjamin
Major work:
Research on free will (p23)

Loftus, Elizabeth
Major work:
False memories (p46–7)

McGurk, Harry
Major work:
Visual and auditory
processing (p21)

Marazziti, Donatella
Major work:
Research on love (p85)

Mehrabian, Albert
Major work:
Research on likeability (p84)

Milgram, Stanley
Major work:
Research on obedience (p96)

Miller, George
Major work:
Research on short-term
memory (p34)

Murray, Henry
Major work:
Thematic apperception (p115)

Oppenheimer, Daniel
Major work:
Research on writing (p53)

Pavlov, Ivan
Major work:
Classical conditioning (p75)

Piaget, Jean
Major work:
Child development (p62–3)

Ramachandran, Vilayanur
Major work:
Behavioral neurology (p26–7)

Rorschach, Hermann
Major work:
Inkblot test (p114–15)

Rotter, Julian
Major work:
Locus of control (p135)

Schwartz, Barry
Major work:
Decision making (p121)

Seligman, Martin
Major work:
Learned Helplessness (p81)

Skinner, Burrhus
Major work:
Operant conditioning (p6, 75)

Snyder, Allan
Major work:
Research using transcranial
magnetic stimulation (p67)

Spearman, Charles
Major work:
Theories on intelligence (p54)

Stack Sullivan, Harry
Major work:
Observed psychoanalysis
(p74)

Stampfl, Thomas
Major work:
Developed "flooding" for
treatment of phobias (p139)

Tajfel, Henri
Major work:
Social identity theory (p94)

Thayer, Robert
Major work:
Reaearch on mood (p73)

Watson, John
Major work:
Behaviorism (p6, 86)

Weiskrantz, Lawrence
Major work:
Research into blindsight (p16)

Wernicke, Carl
Major work:
The localization of
brain function (p56)

Wilson, Timothy
Major work:
The durability bias (p73)

Wolpe, Joseph
Major work:
Developed "systematic
desensitization" for treatment
of phobias (p139)

INDEX

REFERENCES

In most cases throughout this book direct references have been omitted in order to improve the ease of reading. The references and further reading given below are listed in the order that they appear within each chapter.

Chapter 1: Perception and Action

Milner, A.D., Perrett, D.I., Johnston, R.S., Benson, P.J., Jordan, T.R., Heeley, D.W., Bettucci, D., Mortara, F., Mutani, R., Terazzi, E., and Davidson, D.L.W. (1991). Perception and Action in Visual Form Agnosia. *Brain*, 114, 405–428.

Yarrow, K., Haggard, P., Heal, R., Brown, P., and Rothwell, J.C. (2001). Illusory Perceptions of Space and Time Preserve Cross-Saccadic Perceptual Continuity. *Nature*, 414, 302–305.

Zihl, J., Von Cramon, D., and Mai, N. (1983). Selective Disturbance of Movement Vision After Bilateral Brain Damage. *Brain*, 106, 313–340.

Freyd, J.J. and Finke, R.A. (1984). Representational Momentum. *Journal of Experimental Psychology: Learning, Memory & Cognition*, 10, 126–132.

Romi Nijhawan. (2002). Neural Delays, Visual Motion and the Flash-Lag Effect. *Trends in Cognitive Sciences*, 6, 387–393.

Guegen, N. (2007). Courtship Compliance: The Effect of Touch on Women's Behaviour. *Social Influence*, 2, 81–97.

Lewald, J. (2007). More Accurate Sound Localisation Induced by Short-Term Light Deprivation. *Neuropsychologia*, 45, 1215–1222.

Willich, S.N., Wegscheider, Stallman, M., and Keil, T. (2006). Noise Burden and the Risk of Myocardial Infarction. *European Heart Journal*, 27, 276–282.

Mcgurk, H. & MacDonald, J. (1976). Hearing Lips and Seeing Voices. *Nature*, 264, 746–748.

Sacks, O. (1991). *Seeing Voices: A Journey into the Land of the Deaf.* London: Picador.

Blakemore, S-J., Wolpert, D.M., and Frith, C.D. (1998). Central Cancellation of Self-Produced Tickle Sensation. *Nature Neuroscience*, 1, 635–640.

Libet B., Gleason C.A., Wright E.W., and Pearl D.K. (1983). Time of Conscious Intention to Act in Relation to Onset of Cerebral Activity (Readiness–Potential). The Unconscious Initiation of a Freely Voluntary Act. *Brain*, 106, 623–642.

Ward, J. (2003). State of the Art—Synaesthesia. *The Psychologist*, 16, 196–199.

Lehrer, J. (2007). Blue Monday, Green Thursday. *New Scientist*, 194, 48–51.

Simner, J. and Ward, J. (2006). The Taste of Words on the Tip of the Tongue. *Nature*, 444, 438.

Ramachandran, V. S., Rogers-Ramachandran, D.C., and Stewart, M. (1992). Perceptual Correlates of Massive Cortical Reorganization. *Science*, 258, 1159–1160.

Ramachandran, V. S., Rogers-Ramachandran, D.C., and Cobb, C. (1995). Touching the Phantom. *Nature*, 377, 489–490.

Chapter 2: Memory

Kandel, E.R. and Schwartz, J.H. (1982). Molecular Biology of Learning: Modulation of Transmitter Release. *Science*, 218, 433–443.

Miller, G. A. (1956). The Magical Number Seven, Plus or Minus Two: Some Limits on Our Capacity for Processing Information. *Psychological Review*, 63, 81–97.

Conchiglia, G., Rocca, G.D., and Grossi, D. (2007). On a Peculiar Environmental Dependency Syndrome in a Case with Frontal-Temporal Damage: Zelig-Like Syndrome. *Neurocase*, 13, 1–5.

Tests For "Face-blindness" Reveal Disorder May Not Be So Rare. March 25, 2008 www.sciencedaily.com

Lewis, M.B. (2006). Eye-Witnesses Should not do Cryptic Crosswords Prior to Identity Parades. *Perception*, 35, 1433–1436.

Vince, G. Rewriting Your Past. *New Scientist*, 188, 32–35.

Vaiva, G., Ducricq, F., Jezequel, K., Averland, B., Lestavel, P., Brunet, A., and Marmar, C.R. (2003). Immediate Treatment with Propranolol Decreases Postraumatic Stress Disorder Two Months After Trauma. *Biological Psychiatry*, 54, 947–949.

Brunet, A., Orr, S.P., Tremblay, J., Robertson, K., Nader, K., and Pitman, R.K. (2008). Effect of Post-Retrieval Propranolol on Psychophysiologic Responding During Subsequent Script-Driven Traumatic Imagery in Post-Traumatic Stress Disorder. *Journal of Psychiatric Research*, 42, 503–506.

Maguire, E.A., Valentine, E.R., Wilding, J.M. & Kapur, N. (2002). Routes to Remembering: The Brains Behind Superior Memory. *Nature Neuroscience*, 6, 90 – 95.

Wilson, R.S., Mendes de Leon, C.F., Barnes, L.L., Schneider, J.A., Bienias, J.L., Evans, D.A., and Bennett, D.A. (2002). Participation in Cognitively Stimulating Activities and Risk of Incident Alzheimer Disease. *JAMA*, 287, 742–748.

Keetley, V., Wood, A.W., Spong, J., and Stough, C. (2006). Neuropsychological Sequelae of Digital Mobile Phone Exposure in Humans. *Neuropsychologia*, 44, 1843–1848.

Parker, A., and Dagnall, N. (2007). Effects of Bilateral Eye Movements on Gist Based False Recognition in the DRM Paradigm. *Brain and Cognition*, 63, 221–225.

Jyoo, S-S., Hu, P.T., Gujar, N., Jolesz, F.A., and Walker, M.P. (2007). A Deficit in the Ability to Form New Human Memories Without Sleep. *Nature Neuroscience*, 10, 385–392.

Sahakian, B. and Morein-Zamir, S. Professor's Little Helper. *Nature* 450, 1157–1159.

Hamani, C., McAndrews, M.P., Cohn, M., Oh, M., Zumsteg, D., Shapiro, C.M., Wennberg, R.A., and Lozano, A.M.. (2008). Memory Enhancement Induced by Hypothalamic/Fornix Deep Brain Stimulation. *Annals of Neurology*, 63, 119–123.

Rohrer, D. and Pashler, H. (2007). Increasing Retention Time Without Increasing Study Time. *Current Directions in Psychological Science*, 16, 183–186.

Wildschut, T., Sedikides, C., Arndt, J., and Routledge, C. (2006). Nostalgia: Content, Triggers, Functions. *Journal of Personality and Social Psychology*, 91, 975–993.

Routledge, C., Arndt, J., Sedikides, C., and Wildschut, T. (2007). A Blast From the Past: The Terror Management Function of Nostalgia. *Journal of Experimental Social Psychology*, 44, 132–140

Peterson, C., Grant, V.V. & Boland, L.D. (2005). Childhood Amnesia in Children and Adolescents: Their Earliest Memories. *Memory*, 13, 622–637.

Neimark, J. (1996). The Diva of Disclosure, Memory Research Elizabeth Loftus. *Psychology Today*, 29, 48–54.

Bernstein, D.M., Laney, C., Morris, E.K., and Loftus, E.F. (2005). False Beliefs About Fattening Foods Can Have Healthy Consequences. *Proceedings of the National Academy of Sciences, USA*, 102, 13724–31

Manning, C. G. (2000). Imagining Inflation with Post-Test Delays: How Long Will It Last? Unpublished doctoral dissertation, University of Washington.

Chapter 3: Cognition

Riis, J., Loewenstein, G., Baron, J., Jepson, C., Fagerlin, A., and Ubel, P.A. (2005). Ignorance of Hedonic Adaptation to Hemodialysis: A Study Using Ecological Momentary Assessment. *Journal of Experimental Psychology: General*, 134, 3–9.

Myers, D.G. (2002). *Intuition: Its Powers and Perils*. New Haven: Yale University Press.

Small, D.A., Loewenstein, G., and Slovic, P. (2007). Sympathy and Callousness: The Impact of Deliberative Thought on Donations to Identifiable and Statistical Victims. *Organisational Behaviour and Human Decision Processes*, 102, 143–153.

Geier, A.B., Rozin, P., and Doros, G. (2006). Unit Bias. A New Heuristic that Helps Explain the Effect of Portion Size on Food Intake. *Psychological Science*, 17, 521–525.

Alter, A., and Oppenheimer, D.M. (2006). Predicting Short-Term Stock Fluctuations by Using Processing Fluency. *Proceedings of the National Academy of Sciences, USA*, 103, 9369–9372.

Gregory, R.L. (Ed.) (2004). *Oxford Companion to the Mind*. Oxford: Oxford University Press Books.

Flynn, J.R. (2007). Solving the IQ puzzle. *Scientific American Mind*, 18, 24–31.

Avenanti, A., Bueti, D., Galati, G., and Aglioti, S.M. (2005). Transcranial Magnetic Stimulation Highlights the Sensorimotor Side of Empathy for Pain. *Nature Neuroscience*, 8, 955–960.

Gordon, P. (2004). Numerical Cognition Without Words: Evidence from Amazonia. *Science*, 306, 496-499.

Dehaene, S., Izard, V., Pica, P., and Spelke, E. (2006). Core Knowledge of Geometry in an Amazonian Indigene Group. *Science*, 311, 381–384.

Hespos, S.J. and Spelke, E.S. (2004). Conceptual Precursors to Language. *Nature*, 430, 453–456.

Spinney, L. (2007). The Science of Swearing. *New Scientist*, 196, 51–53.

Kho, K.H., Duffau, H., Gatignol, P., Leijten, F.S.S., Ramsey, N.F., van Rijen, P.C., and Rutten, G-J.M. (2007). Involuntary Language Switching in Two Bilingual Patients During the Wada Test and Intraoperative Electrocortical Stimulation. *Brain and Language*, 101, 31–37.

Atkin, K. and Lorch, M.P. (2006). Hyperlexia in a 4-Year-Old Boy with Autistic Spectrum Disorder. *Journal of Neurolinguistics*, 19, 253–269.

Beilin, H. (1992). Piaget's Enduring Contribution to Developmental Psychology. *Developmental Psychology*, 28, 191–204.

Bowden, E.M., Jung-Beemana, M., Fleck, J., and Kounios, J. (2005). New Approaches to Demystifying Insight. *Trends in Cognitive Science*, 9, 322–328.

Kadosh, R.C., Kadosh, K.C., Schuhmann, T., Kaas, A., Goebel, R., Henik, A., and Sack, A.T. (2007). Virtual Dyscalculia Induced by Parietal-Lobe TMS Impairs Automatic Magnitude Processing. *Current Biology*, 17, 1–5.

Dehaene, S., Bossini, S., and Giraux, P. (1993). The Mental Representation of Parity and Number Magnitude. *Journal of Experimental Psychology: General*, 122, 371–396.

Chapter 4: Affect

Ellis, H.C. and Ashbrook, P.W. (1991) In *Mood and memory: theory, research, and applications*, London: Sage Publications

Blaney, P. H. (1986) Affect and Memory: A Review. *Psychology Bulletin*, 99, 229–246

Thayer, R. E. (1989). *The Biopsychology of Mood and Arousal*.

New York: Oxford University Press.

Thayer, R. E. (1996). *The Origin of Everyday Moods*. New York: Oxford University Press.

Gilbert, D. T., Pinel, E. C., Wilson, T. D., Blumberg, S. J., and Wheatley, T. P. (1998). Immune neglect: A Source of Durability Bias in Affective Forecasting. *Journal of Personality and Social Psychology*, 75, 617–638.

Wilson, T. D. (2002). *Strangers to Ourselves: Discovering the Adaptive Unconscious*. Cambridge, Mass: Harvard University Press.

Ellis, A. and Dryden, W. (2007). *The Practice of Rational Emotive Behavior Therapy*. New York: Springer Publishing.

Beck, A.T., (1975). *Cognitive Therapy and the Emotional Disorders*. Madison: Inernational Universities Press.

Erfani, A., Erfanian, A. (2004). The Effects of Mental Practice and Concentration Skills on EEG Brain Dynamics During Motor Imagery Using Independent Component Analysis. *Engineering in Medicine and Biology Society—26th Annual International Conference of the IEEE*, 1–5, 239–242.

Csikszentmihályi, M. (2008). *Flow: The Psychology of Optimal Experience*. New York: Harper.

Leppanen, J.M. (2004). *Emotion-Cognition Interaction in Recognizing Facial Expressions*. Tampere, Finland: Tampere University Press.

Sprengelmeyer, R., Young, A.W., Calder, A.J., Karnat, A., Lange, H., Homberg, V., Perrett, D.I., and Rowland, D. (1996). Perception of Faces and Emotions: Loss of Disgust in Huntington's Disease. *Brain*, 119, 1647–1665

Abrahamson, L. Y., Seligman, M. E. P., and Teasdale, J. D. (1978). Learned Helplessness in Humans: Critique and Reformulation. *Journal of Abnormal Psychology*, 87, 49–74.

Hamachek, D.E. (1978). Psychodynamics of Normal and Neurotic Perfectionism. *Psychology*, 15, 27–33.

Eich, E. and Suedfeld, P. (1995). Autobiographical Memory and Affect Under Conditions of Reduced Stimulation. *Journal of Environmental Psychology*. 15, 321–26

Jacob, S., McClintock, M. K., Zelano, B., and Ober, C. (2002). Paternally Inherited HLA Alleles are Associated With Women's Choice of Male Odor. *Nature Genetics*, 30, 175–179

Mehrabian, A. (1971). *Silent Messages*. Belmont: Wadsworth.

Marazziti, D., Akiska, H.S., Rossi, A., and Cassano, G.B. (1999). Alteration of the Platelet Serotonin Transporter in Romantic Love. *Psychological Medicine*, 29, 741–745

Watson, J. B. (1913). Psychology as the Behaviorist Views It. *Psychological Review*, 20, 158–177.

Blum, D. (2003). *Love at Goon Park: Harry Harlow and the Science of Affection*. New York: John Wiley & Sons.

Ayduk, O., Downey, G., and Kim, M., (2001). Rejection Sensitivity and Depressive Symptoms in Women. *Personality and Social Psychology Bulletin*, 7, 868–877.

Mayer, J.D. and Salovey, P. (1997). What is Emotional Intelligence? In P. Salovey and D.J. Sluyter (Eds.) *Emotional Development and Emotional Intelligence*. New York: Basic Books.

Lazarus, R., Bernice, N,. (1994) *Passion and Reason: Making Sense of Our Emotions*. New York: Oxford University Press.

Chapter 5: The Social Self

Tajfel, H., Flament, C., Billig, M.G., and Bundy, R.P. (1971). Social Categorisation and Intergroup Behaviour. *European Journal of Social Psychology*, 1, 149–178.

Jones, D. (2007). The Depths of Disgust. *Nature*, 447, 768–771.

Harris, L.T. and Fiske, S.T. (2006). Dehumanising the Lowest of the Low. Neuroimaging Responses to Extreme Out-Groups. *Psychological Science*, 17, 847–853.

Milgram, S. (1963). Behavioral Study of Obedience. *Journal of Abnormal and Social Psychology*, 67, 371–378.

Slater, M., Antley, M., Davison, A., Swapp, D., Guger, C., Barker, C., Pistrang, N., and Sanchez-Vives, M.V. (2006). A Reprise of the Stanley Milgram Obedience Experiments. *PloS One*, 1, e39.

Diehl, M. and Stroebe, W. (1987). Productivity Loss in Brainstorming Groups: Toward the Solution of a Riddle. *Journal of Personality and Social Psychology*, 53, 497–509.

Nijstad, B.A., Stroebe, W., and Lodewijkx, H.F.M. (2006). The Illusion of Group Productivity: A Reduction of Failures Explanation. *European Journal of Social Psychology*, 36, 31–48.

Fay, D., Borrill, C., Amir, Z., Haward, R., and West, M.A. (2006). Getting the most out of multidisciplinary teams: A Multi-Sample Study of Team Innovation in Health Care. *Journal of Occupational and Organizational Psychology*, 79, 553–567.

Nemeth, C.J. and Ormiston, M. (2007). Creative Idea Generation: Harmony Versus Stimulation. *European Journal of Social Psychology*, 524–535.

Laughlin, P.R., Hatch, E.C., Silver, J.S., and Boh, L. (2006). Groups Perform Better Than the Best Individuals on Letters-to-Numbers Problems: Effects of Group Size. *Journal of Personality and Social Psychology*, 90, 644–651.

Choi, H-K. and Thompson, L. (2005). Old Wine in a New Bottle: Impact of Membership Change on Group Creativity. *Organisational Behaviour and Human Decision Processes*, 98, 121–132.

Maddux, W.W., Mullen, E., and Galinsky, A.D. (2008). Chameleons Bake Bigger Pies and Take Bigger Pieces: Strategic Behavioural Mimicry Facilitates Negotiation Outcomes. *Journal of Experimental Social Psychology*, 44, 461–468.

van Baaren, R.B., Holland, R.W., Kawakami, K., and van Knippenberg, A. (2004). Mimicry and Prosocial Behaviour. *Psychological Science*, 15, 71–74.

Wu, S. and Keysar, B. (2007). The Effect of Culture on Perspective Taking. *Psychological Science*, 18, 600–606.

Leung, A.K-Y. and Cohen, D. (2007). The Soft Embodiment of Culture: Camera Angles and Motion Through Time and Space. *Psychological Science*, 18, 824–830.

Hedden, T., Ketay, S., Aron, A., Markus, H.R., and Gabrieli, J.D.E. (2008). Cultural Influences on Neural Substrates of Attentional Control. *Psychological Science*, 19, 12–17.

Kaplan, R.M. and Kronick, R.G. (2006). Marital Status and Longevity in the United States Population. *Journal of Epidemiology and Community Health*, 60, 760–765.

Sedikides, C. and Kumashiro, M. (2005). On the Resource Function of Relationships: Close Positive Relationships as a Dissonance Reduction Mechanism. Unpublished manuscript. University of Southampton.

Oswald, D.L. and Clark, E.M. (2003). Best Friends Forever?: High School Best Friendships and the Transition to College. *Personal Relationships*, 10, 187–196.

Slatcher, R.B. and Pennebaker, J.W. (2006). How do I Love Thee? Let Me Count the Words. The Social Effects of Expressive Writing. *Psychological Science*, 17, 660–664.

Sprecher, S. (2001). Equity and Social Exchange in Dating Couples: Associations with Satisfaction, Commitment, and Stability. *Journal of Marriage and the Family*, 63, 599–613.

Gottman, J.M., Coan, J., Carrere, S., and Swanson, C. (1998). Predicting Marital Happiness and Stability from Newlywed Interactions. *Journal of Marriage and the Family*, 60, 5–22.

Bechara, B., Damasio, H., Tranel, D., and Damasio, A.R. (1997). Deciding Advantageously Before Knowing the Advantageous Strategy. *Science*, 275, 1293–1295.

Koenigs, M., Young, L., Adolphs, R., Tranel, D., Cushman, F., Hauser, M., and Damasio, A. (2007). Damage to the Prefrontal Cortex Increases Utilitarian Moral Judgements. *Nature*, 446, 908–911.

Baron-Cohen, S. (2008). Theories of the Autistic Mind. *The Psychologist*, 21, 112–116.

Chapter 6: Personality

Nettle, D. (2007). *Personality. What Makes You the Way You Are.* Oxford: Oxford University Press

Reicher, S.D. Haslam, A., and Platow, M.J. (2007). The New Psychology of Leadership. *Scientific American Mind*, 18, 22–29.

Rule, N.O. and Ambady, N. (2008). The Face of Success: Inferences From Chief Executive Officers' Appearance Predict Company Profits. *Psychological Science*, 19, 109–111.

Fragale, A.R. (2006). The Power of Powerless Speech: The Effects of Speech Style and Task Interdependence on Status Conferral. *Organisational Behaviour and Human Decision Processes*, 101, 243–261.

Andeweg, R.B. and Van Den Berg, S.B. (2003). Linking Birth Order to Political Leadership: The Impact of Parents of Sibling Interaction? *Political Psychology*, 24, 605–623.

O'Connor, R.C. and O'Connor, D.B. (2003). Predicting Hopelessness and Psychological Distress: The Role of Perfectionism and Coping. *Journal of Counselling Psychology*, 50, 362–372.

Schwartz, B. (2004). The Tyranny of Choice. *Scientific American*, 290, 70–5.

Kihlstrom, J.F. (2005). Dissociative Disorders. *Annual Review of Clinical Psychology*, 1, 227–253.

Alwin, N., Blackburn, R., Davidson, K., Hilton, M., Logan, C., and Shine, J. (2006). *Understanding Personality Disorder: A Professional Practice Board Report by the British Psychological Society.* Leicester: British Psychological Society.

Solms, M. (2004). Freud Returns. *Scientific American*, 290, 82–8.

Anderson, M.C. and Green, C. (2001). Suppressing Unwanted Memories by Executive Control. *Nature*, 410, 131–134.

Chapter 7: Stress and Anxiety

Molinari, V., Khanna, P. (1981) Locus of Control and Its Relationship to Anxiety and Depression. *Journal of Personality Assessment*, 45, 314–3.

Njus, D.M. and Brockway, J.H. (1999). Perceptions of Competence and Locus of Control for Positive and Negative Outcomes. *Personality and Individual Differences*, 26, 531–548

At Least 96 Killed in Nightclub Inferno. February 2003, cnn. com

Diagnostic and Statistical Manual of Mental Disorders, Fourth Edition (DSM-IV). American Psychiatric Association.

LeDoux J. (1998). Fear and the Brain: Where Have We Been, and Where are We Going? *Biological Psychiatry*, 44, 1229–38

Skre, I., Onstad, S., Torgersen, S., Lygren, S., and Kringlen, E. (2000). The Heritability of Common Phobic Fear: A Twin Study of a Clinical Sample. *Journal of Anxiety Disorders*, 6, 549–562.

Parslow, R.A., and Jorm, A.F. (2007). Pretrauma and Posttrauma Neurocognitive Functioning and PTSD Symptoms in a Community Sample of Young Adults. *American Journal of Psychiatry*, 164, 509–515.

Benson, H. (1984). *Beyond the Relaxation Response.* New York: Times Books.

Linden, C. (2008) *The Linden Method: The Anxiety and Panic Attacks Elimination Solution.* Idaho: Lifewise Publishing.

Chapter 8: Sleep

Goode, E. (2003). When the Brain Disrupts the Night. *NY Times.*

Siegel, J.M., A tribute to Nathaniel Kleitman. www.npi.ucla.edu

Jarrett, D.B., Miewald, J. M., and Kupfer, D. J. (1990). Recurrent depression is associated with a persistent reduction in sleep-related growth hormone. *Archives of General Psychiatry*, 47, 113–118.

Rochlen, A.B.; Ligiero, D.P.; Hill, C.E.; Heaton, K.J. (1999). Effects of Training in Dream Recall and Dream Interpretation Skills on Dream Recall, Attitudes, and Dream Interpretation Outcome. *Journal of Counseling Psychology*, 46, 27–34.

Rosenfeld, M. (November 1998). Van Gogh's Madness The Diagnosis Debate Lives On *Washington Post.*

Martinez, R. (2007). Changing a Nightmare's Script. (The Dream Zone). *Addiction Professional*, 5, 42.

Wood , S. and Bettman, J. (2007) Predicting Happiness: How Normative Feeling Rules Influence (and Even Reverse) Durability Bias. *Journal of Counseling Psychology*, 17, 188–201.

Coren, S. (1996). *Sleep Thieves.* New York: Simon and Schuster.

CREDITS

Dr. Christian Jarrett is creator and editor of the British Psychological Society's award-winning Research Digest blog and staff writer on *The Psychologist* magazine. He's author of *The Rough Guide to Psychology*, editor of *30-Second Psychology*, and has written for *New Scientist, Wired, The Times, The Guardian,* and more. Christian contributed the Introduction, Chapters 1, 2, 3, 5 and 6, and all the exercises.

He's on Twitter @Psych_Writer.

Christian is indebted to his wife Jude and his mother Linda for their support, and most of all, for believing that he could do it. He'd like to thank James Evans for asking him to get on board in the first place, James Beattie for managing the project as it progressed, and Matt Pagett for the fun illustrations (redrawn by Tony Seddon in the revised edition). Lastly, Christian would like to acknowledge the hard work and creativity of the psychologists who conducted the many experiments and formulated the theories written about within these pages.

Joannah Ginsburg is a psychotherapist who has provided therapy to survivors of the attacks on the World Trade Center, as well as having worked in private practice, hospital, clinic, and school settings throughout the United States. She specializes in the management of stress, anxiety, depression, corporate issues, and marital struggles. She has also been a features reporter for the *Wall Herald*, and is a regular contributor to psychology publications and newsletters. Joannah contributed Chapters 4, 7 and 8.

Joannah would like to thank all the people who have allowed her, as their therapist, into their innermost worlds for everything she has learned from them. Also Keyvan and her family for their support and patience, her fellow psychotherapists at Lifeworks Counseling for the creative energy and collaborative environment, Steven Nixon, mentors of the past and present, and James Evans and James Beattie at Quid Publishing for providing the opportunity, framework, and inspiration.

Images

All illustrations © Quid Publishing.
All photos public domain, except:
page 21 © Shutterstock | Ljupco Smokovski
page 26 courtesy of V.S. Ramachandran
page 33 (top) © Shutterstock | cbpix
page 33 (bottom) © Shutterstock | Stephen Rees
page 46 courtesy of Elizabeth Loftus
page 49 © Shutterstock | Anthony Correia
page 57 © Shutterstock | AMC Photography
page 61 © Shutterstock | Svetlana Lukienko
page 62 courtesy of Roland Zumbühl
(www.picswiss.ch)
page 81 © Shutterstock | Sergii Figurnyi

page 86 © Shutterstock | Dan Kelleher
page 91 © Shutterstock | Eric Isselee
page 101 © Shutterstock | Viorel Sima
page 104 © Shutterstock | lculig
page 105 © Shutterstock | Chamille White
page 106 courtesy of Antonio Damasio
page 115 © Shutterstock | albund
page 137 © Shutterstock | Piotr Wawrzyniuk
page 142 courtesy of the Benson-Henry Institute of Mind Body Medicine
page 145 © Shutterstock | Eillen
page 159 © Shutterstock | Coprid
page 162 © Creative Commons | CaptainPsychology
page 165 © Shutterstock | Warren Goldswain